Shortcuts

FOR
TEACHING
PHONICS

Cover by Janet Skiles

Copyright © Good Apple, Inc., 1990

ISBN No. 0-86653-514-4

Printing No. 98

Good Apple
A Division of Frank Schaffer Publications, Inc.
23740 Hawthorne Boulevard
Torrance, CA 90505-5927

By Flora Joy

Illustrated by Pat Harroll

Dedicated to Jane Montgomery

2

Table of Contents

GA1143

Do you
waste valuable
time preparing dozens
of separate phonics activities
for one-time use? Spend only minutes
preparing four different attractive,
exciting, permanent, portable,
flexible, easy-to-use activities
which young learners beg to
do! The work has already
been done for you. Just
photocopy or cut from
the text dozens of
special multiuse
phonics pages.
Hours of fun and
learning are in store for all!

GA1143

SECTION 1
PHONICS OVERVIEW

The purpose of teaching phonics in today's classrooms is to equip learners with a lifetime method of pronouncing unknown words. When faced with unfamiliar written words, readers need one or more decoding systems. Phonics is one such system. Simply stated, phonics is a method of determining the sounds represented by the written letters in printed words.

An examination of professional research findings and recommendations regarding the teaching of phonics reveals thousands of pages of information and hundreds of "rules" to consider. Most classroom teachers are not provided the time to study this information, to decide how it relates to their classrooms, and then to develop corresponding activities for helping their students build needed phonics skills. Therefore, the text *Shortcuts for Teaching Phonics* was prepared.

Before one considers "shortcuts" for teaching these skills, however, one must understand at least a few basic principles regarding the relationships of sounds and letters. The following pages, therefore, provide a very simplistic overview of these skills.

The spoken language consists of two classifications of sound utterances: vowel sounds and consonant sounds. The following pages provide explanations of these two categories of sounds in addition to how phonics rules and generalizations are formed and taught.

Vowel Sounds

There are fifteen vowel sounds in America's major dialects. Five of these sounds are referred to in most elementary textbooks as "long vowel sounds" and five as "short vowel sounds." (Note that the words **long** and **short** are confusing terms because they have **no** association with the **length** of the sounds or the letters representing these sounds. The five remaining vowel sounds were not given "names.")

Long Vowel Sounds

The five long vowel sounds are spoken the same as their letter names:

- \ā* as in **bait**
- \ē\ as in **beet**
- \ī\ as in **bite**
- \ō\ as in **boat**
- \yü\ as in **beautiful**

(Note that the "long u" is actually a combination of the consonant sound \y\ and the vowel sound \ü\. The letter **u** and the word **you** have the same **two** sounds: \yü\. This can cause confusion among young learners already struggling with a complex decoding system.)

The long vowel sounds occur in the initial, medial, and final positions of words or syllables. Examples are **ate, plate, play; eat, meat, he; I'll, nine, buy; oat, bone, go; use, mule, pew.**

In order to write a **sound on paper, diacritical symbols are used. Since many different systems are in print, this document will use those found in the Merriam Webster's dictionaries.*

Short Vowel Sounds

The five short vowel sounds are as follows:

- \a\ as in **bat**
- \e\ as in **bet**
- \i\ as in **bit**
- \ä\ as in **bottle**
- \ə\ as in **but**

(Note that the "short u" sound is often referred to as the **schwa** sound, generally written as an upside down e.) The short sounds occur in the initial and medial positions of words or

GA1143

syllables, but they rarely occur in the final positions. Examples are **at, mat; edge, met; it, hip; odd, hot; up, cut.**

Other Vowel Sounds

The five remaining "unnamed" vowel sounds are as follows:
- \ u̇ \ as in **foot**
- \ ȯ \ as in **awe**
- \ ər \ as in **her**
- \ ȯi \ as in **boy**
- \ au̇ \ as in **out**

The last two of these sounds (\ ȯi \ and \ au̇\) are called **diphthongs.** A vowel diphthong is an utterance which causes the articulators (tongue, lips, etc.) to move from the position of making one vowel sound to the position of making another vowel sound **within the single enunciation.** (Try saying "OW!" **without** moving your articulators. The utterance "OW," however, is considered **one** sound rather than two.) In many American dialects, the long **i** sound is also a diphthong. It is possible for other vowel sounds to be diphthongs (or even triphthongs).

(Note that the sound \ ü \ was not listed as an additional vowel sound. This is the vowel sound heard in the "long u" utterance. However, many words contain the sound \ ü \ without the consonant \ y \ preceding it, such as **boot** or **suit**.)

Vowel Letters

Vowel letters are any letters used to record (or help record) a vowel sound. These are written either as single vowel letters or as vowel digraphs. These vowel letters are **a, e, i, o, u,** and sometimes **w** and **y.**

Single Vowel Letters

When only **one** letter is used to record a vowel sound, it is called a single vowel letter.

These six single vowel letters are as follows:
- **a** as in **at**
- **e** as in **me**
- **i** as in **it**
- **o** as in **odd**
- **u** as in **up**
- **y** as in **by**

(Note that **w** is not used as a **single** vowel letter.)

Vowel Digraphs

When **two** letters are used to record **one** vowel sound, they are called vowel digraphs. (This term can be more easily learned by remembering that **di-** means **two,** and **-graph-** means **to write.**) The following are some commonly used vowel digraphs:
- **ai** as in **mail**
- **ay** as in **say**
- **ea** as in **eat**
- **ee** as in **meet**
- **ey** as in **key**
- **ie** as in **pie**
- **oa** as in **oat**
- **oo** as in **foot**
- **ow** as in **snow**

There are many additional digraphs which are less frequently used, such as **uy** in **buy** or **uu** in **vacuum.** Note that two vowel letters occurring together in a word will not *always* be a digraph. Words such as **skiing, neon,** and **diet** do not have digraphs because each of the two vowel letters represents a separate single vowel sound. Note also that vowel trigraphs (three vowel letters representing one sound) exist: **eye, awe, gracious.** However, these do not need to be discussed in elementary phonics classrooms.

GA1143

Consonant Sounds

The term **consonant** is difficult to define for young learners. Perhaps it is a cop-out to say, "consonant sounds are any sounds (occurring in words) which are not vowel sounds." A concept of consonant sounds may be more accurately formed after much experience and practice. Consonant sounds may occur as single sounds or as blends.

Single Consonant Sounds

Single consonant sounds may occur in the initial or final positions of **syllables** (and in medial positions of **words** with more than one syllable). The following are single consonant sounds which are easier for young learners:

- \b\ as in **be, rib**
- \d\ as in **do, hid**
- \f\ as in **fee, if**
- \h\ as in **he**
- \l\ as in **lie, eel**
- \j\ as in **job**

(See "soft **g**" in later section.)

- \m\ as in **me, am**
- \n\ as in **no, on**
- \p\ as in **pie, hip**
- \r\ as in **row, star**
- \s\ as in **so, bus**

(See "soft **c**" in later section.)

- \t\ as in **to, at**

(Note that the letter **h** is not a single consonant letter if it occurs at the end of a syllable. In that position it is either part of a consonant digraph in words such as **enough** or it is part of a "silent team" as in the word **sigh**.)

The following four single consonant sounds are often presented after several of the above sounds have been studied:

- \v\ as in **van, give**
- \w\ as in **we**
- \y\ as in **ye**

- \z\ as in **zoo, buzz, his**

(Note that the letters **w** and **y** do not represent consonant sounds when they appear at the **ends** of syllables. In this position the letters **w** and **y** are vowel letters.)

The letter **c** is generally taught as representing "soft" (\s\) and "hard" (\k\) sounds. These are as follows:

- \s\ as in **cell, nice**
- \k\ as in **can, picnic**

(Note that these sounds may also be spelled with the letters **s** and **k** in addition to the **c**.)

The letter **g** is also taught as representing "soft" (\j\) and "hard" (\g\) sounds. These are as follows:

- \j\ as in **gel, edge**
- \g\ as in **go, egg, pig**

(Note that the sound \j\ is spelled with both the letters **g** and **j**.)

Additional single consonant sounds are discussed later with consonant digraphs.

GA1143

Consonant Blends

A consonant blend is a combination of two or more consonant sounds which occur "side by side" as a syllable is spoken. They do *not blend* into **one** sound. It is possible to voice each separate sound in all consonant blends. It is important to remember that the term **consonant blend** refers to **sounds** rather than letters, although in many cases the blends will be spelled with one letter for each sound.

When consonant blends are introduced to young learners, it is easier to begin with some from the following list of initial blends:

- \ bl \ as in **blue**
- \ br \ as in **bring**
- \ dr \ as in **dry**
- \ fl \ as in **fly**
- \ fr \ as in **fry**
- \ gl \ as in **glue**
- \ gr \ as in **gray**
- \ pl \ as in **play**
- \ pr \ as in **pray**
- \ sl \ as in **slow**
- \ sm \ as in **small**
- \ sn \ as in **snow**
- \ sp \ as in **spot**
- \ st \ as in **stay**
- \ tr \ as in **try**

The above are both frequently used and are generally spelled with the letters which diacritically represent their sounds. The following are less common and/or have alternative spelling choices:

- \ kl \ as in **claw**
- \ kr \ as in **cry**
- \ dw \ as in **Dwight**
- \ sk \ as in **scan**
- \ sw \ as in **sweet**
- \ tw \ as in **twinkle**

A special blend (depending upon dialect) is one typically spelled with the letters **wh**. Note that in dialects which voice this as a blend, the \ h \ is uttered first, followed by \ w \—the reverse of the written representation. Dialects voicing the **wh-** spellings as *one* sound generally omit the \ h \.

- \ hw \ as in **why**

Some initial consonant blends have three sounds and are also represented by three letters, such as the following:

- \ skr \ as in **scream**
- \ spl \ as in **splash**
- \ spr \ as in **spring**
- \ str \ as in **street**

Some consonant blends which are more difficult for young learners contain consonant digraphs in their spellings:

- \ kr \ as in **Christmas**
- \ sk \ as in **school**
- \ thr \ as in **throw**

Consonant blends also occur at the *ends* of syllables. These are easier to grasp when the blends are ones which also occur at the beginnings of syllables, such as the following:

- \ sp \ as in **wasp**
- \ st \ as in **fist**
- \ sk \ as in **ask**

Consonant blends which do *not* also occur in the initial positions of syllables, such as the following, are more difficult to master:

- \ kt \ as in **act**
- \ ld \ as in **held**
- \ lb \ as in **bulb**
- \ nd \ as in **hand**
- \ rm \ as in **harm**
- \ rn \ as in **horn**

Consonant blends sometimes occur at the ends of syllables which have the letters **-ed** added to the root word, such as the following:

- \ kt \ as in **picked**
- \ bd \ as in **rubbed**
- \ sht \ as in **washed**

GA1143

Other words containing difficult consonant blends may be taught as sight words or with corresponding phonics generalizations. Some examples follow:

- \ kw \ as in **quiet**
- \ fy \ as in **few**
- \ vy \ as in **view**
- \ ks \ as in **fox**

Consonant Letters

A consonant letter is any letter of the alphabet which is used (alone or in combination with other letters) to record a consonant sound. These are written either as single consonant letters or consonant digraphs. These letters used are **b, c, d, f, g, h, j, k, l, m, n, p, q, r, s, t, v, w, x, y, z.**

Single Consonant Letters

When only one letter is used to record a consonant sound, it is called a single consonant letter. Each of those listed above may be used as a single consonant letter.

Consonant Digraphs

When **two** consonant letters are used to record **one** consonant sound, they are called consonant digraphs. The following are some consonant digraphs used in the initial positions of syllables:

- **ch** as in **chair, chef, chorus**
- **ph** as in **phone**
- **sh** as in **shop**
- **th** as in **thin, then**

Note that the printed digraph will not always represent the *same* consonant sound. Examples appear in the different sounds represented by **ch** and **th**.

Some consonant digraphs used in the final positions of syllables are as follows:

- **ch** as in **perch, ache**
- **ph** as in **graph**
- **sh** as in **wash**
- **th** as in **with, bathe**
- **gh** as in **cough**
- **ng** as in **sing**

Note that some sources classify **wh-** as a digraph since some dialects utter this as only one sound. Others also include letter combinations containing silent letters, such as **know, gnaw,** etc. These may be more easily taught as a "silent **k**" or a "silent **g**." A few sources also include words having double consonant letters, such as **all** or **egg**. It is generally easier for young learners if these words are not "labeled" as digraphs, even though they do technically fit the definition.

*Special note: Single consonant letters, blends, and digraphs are easily taught in the initial positions of words and syllables. In the final positions they are usually taught by using **phonograms**. A phonogram is a cluster of letters, usually one or more vowel letters followed by one or more consonant letters. See later sections for examples and activities.*

Phonics Rules

One of the most controversial topics in the teaching of phonics involves which "rules" to teach. Few authorities agree on an identical list to be used for primary grades. When rules are "taught" to young learners, the goal should be for these principles to be *applied* rather than *recited*. Overkill should be avoided at all costs. After a few rules (which have high frequency of application) have been internalized (NOT memorized), learners should be placed in situations where they will WANT to read through exciting experiences such as stories, games, and practical life-coping experiences.

GA1143

The attempt of this document will, therefore, be to identify a *few* phonics generalizations which will help young readers *get started* with goals of **wanting to read, enjoying reading, and reading for information and pleasure!**

Many decoding systems begin with generalizations such as "The letter **b** usually represents the sound \b\ as in **boy** and **rib.**" These generalizations are reflected in the earlier portions of this document and are not repeated here. *In addition* to these earlier concepts, the following rules should be included as part of an on-going decoding program.

Rule 1: In a (C+)VC pattern, try the short vowel sound. Examples are **hat, pet, hit, hot,** and **hut.** The C is the abbreviation for **consonant letter**, the V for **vowel letter.** The + means that more than one letter may appear. Parentheses indicate **optional** letters.

Note that these rules use the word "try." *Good phonics instruction employs a **logical guessing strategy**. Learners should "try" a sound and voice it aloud in an unknown word. If that word does not "sound correct" or does not fit contextually, then a different (logical) sound should be attempted. When possible, these unknown words should occur in phrases or sentences.*

Rule 2: In a C(+)V pattern, try the long vowel sound. Examples are **we,** and **go.** (Some exceptions are **do** and **to.** Teach these two words early as sight words and explain that they are among the few which do not follow this rule.)

Rule 3: In the (C+)VCe pattern, try the long vowel sound. Examples are **hate, Pete, kite, hope,** and **cute.** (This is frequently referred to as the "final silent **e** rule." Some exceptions are **glove, one,** and **machine.**)

Rule 4: When immediately followed by the letters **e, i,** or **y,** the letter **c** will generally repre-sent the \s\ sound and the **g** will represent the \j\ sound. These sounds are often called "soft." Examples are **cell, city, cycle, gem, gin,** and **gym.** (Unfortunately, **get** and **give** are exceptions to this rule and can confuse learners if not taught as exceptions.)

In other cases, the "hard" sounds associated with the letters **c** and **g** will be voiced. Examples are **cake, cot, cut, pick, picnic, gate, got, gut, pig,** and **ugly.**

*This principle can be **of lifetime value** when mature readers try to pronounce words such as **analogous** (hard g) and **analogize** (soft g), or when deciding on how to **spell** words such as **noticeable** or **picnicking**. Note that the **e** is retained in **noticeable** so the **c** will not be followed by the letter **a**, and a **k** is added before the **ing** in **picnicking** so the hard sound of the **c** will be protected. This generalization works with thousands of words encountered daily by adult readers/spellers.*

Rule 5: When appearing at the **end** of syllables, the letters **w** and **y** are vowel letters. The letter **y** may stand alone as a vowel letter (**by, my**) or may be part of a vowel digraph (**pay, key**). The letter **w** will not stand alone as a vowel letter, but may be part of a vowel digraph (**saw, snow, view**). At the beginning of syllables, the letters **w** and **y** will usually represent consonant sounds.

Rule 6: The letters **tion** and **sion** will generally represent \shən\, as in **nation** or **tension.**

A **multitude** of additional "rules" may be taught. Use good judgment in the selection of added phonics rules. Try to make phonics/reading classes exciting and fun! The activities on the following pages are provided for this purpose. Each has a separate explanation of skills, objectives, and preparation instructions.

HAVE FUN!

GA1143

SECTION 2
BIG LETTER PHONICS ACTIVITIES

A variety of activities with large letters may be used to help students master basic phonics principles. The materials on pages 15-46 may be prepared quickly and easily for this purpose. Below are some suggestions.

Single Letter Activities

The cards found on pages 15-31 may be used as **single letter activities** for teaching phonics.

Single Initial Consonant Activities

Global Instructional Objective: The learner will identify pictorial representations of words which begin with selected single initial consonant sounds.

Procedure: Photocopy pages 15-16. Trim each separate letter card at the outside solid border. Mount each card onto a larger piece of heavy paper. If desired, protect each card with laminating film or clear self-adhesive paper.

For one-on-one instruction, the learner may point to the words which begin with the indicated consonant letter. The instructor will indicate the correct answers as these responses occur.

For an **individual self-correcting** activity, puncture the black dots appearing near each picture with an object such as an ice pick. On the *backs* of the cards draw a circle around each small puncture which corresponds to the **correct answers only**. Users of the activity cards will be instructed to gently insert their pencil point only through those dots near pictures which begin with the large letter shown on the card. To determine the accuracy of responses, the card may be turned over while the pencil point is still inserted. Circled items will indicate correct responses. The following drawings show both sides of a sample prepared card.

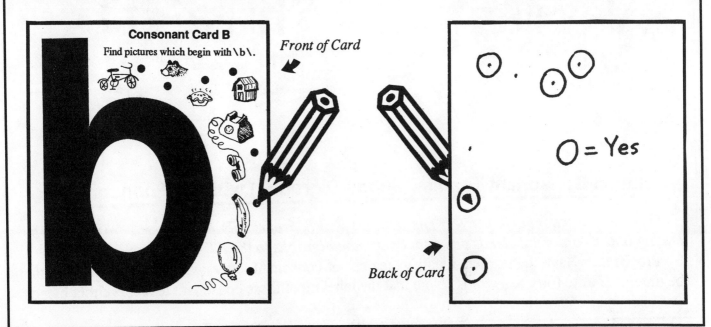

11

GA1143

Vowel Activities

Global Instructional Objective: The learner will identify pictorial representations of words which contain the long and the short vowel sounds.

Procedure: Prepare and use pages 27-31 in the same manner as suggested for the above activity. Learners will need to be aware that five cards have pictures for the short sounds and five for the long sounds.

Single Initial Consonants with the AT Phonogram

Global Instructional Objective: The learners will appropriately pronounce words (or syllables) formed by adding single initial consonant letters to the AT phonogram.

A phonogram is a cluster of letters generally forming numerous words when initial consonant sounds are added.

Procedure: For this activity the cards prepared for the above exercises may be used. If the surrounding pictures shown on these cards are not wanted, **the dark letters only** may be cut out from photocopies and mounted onto heavy paper. Begin the activity by asking two students to hold the **a** and **t** cards (at the front of the classroom) to form the word **at**. Assign thirteen more students to stand at the side of the room and hold the letter cards **b, c, d, f, g, h, k l, m, n, p, r,** and **s**. (Fewer letters may be used, if desired.) *One at a time* a "consonant letter" walks to the beginning of **at**. While this new word or syllable is revealed, ask all students (both those participating and those seated) to simultaneously voice this word (or syllable). For letter combinations which do not form real words, such as **lat**, ask, "If this were a *syllable* in a real word, how would it be pronounced?"

*Words (or syllables) formed with the suggested letters are **bat, cat, dat, fat, gat, hat, kat, lat, mat, nat, pat, rat,** and **sat.***

Initial Consonant Teams (Blends/Digraphs) with AT Phonogram

Global Instructional Objective: The learners will appropriately pronounce words formed by adding initial consonant blends or initial consonant digraphs to the AT phonogram.

Procedure: Have the learners identify "teams" of consonant letters which can be added to the beginning of **at** to form real words. Note that the labeling of these consonant teams as either blends

12

GA1143

or digraphs is not essential. The word *team* communicates the process quite effectively. Should a real word be formed which is unfamiliar to some in the class, have one or more students use the word or explain its meaning.

Possible words for this activity: **brat, chat, drat, flat, gnat, spat, splat, slat,** *and* **scat.** *Note that an extra t in the single letter list can add words such as* **that.** *It is possible for additional terms such as* **frat** *to be suggested. Discuss as desired.*

Single Initial Consonants with the ATE Phonogram

Global Instructional Objective: The learners will appropriately pronounce words (or syllables) formed by adding single initial consonant letters to the ATE phonogram. Through the addition of the letter **e** *onto the end of* **at,** *students will experience the "final silent* **e***" phonics principle.*

Procedure: Proceed through this activity as suggested with the one entitled "Single Initial Consonants with the AT Phonogram."

Initial Consonant Teams (Blends/Digraphs) with the ATE Phonogram

Global Instructional Objective: The learners will appropriately pronounce words formed by adding initial consonant blends or initial consonant digraphs to the ATE phonogram.

Procedures: Proceed as suggested in a similar activity above.

Possible words are **plate, grate, slate, crate,** *and* **skate.** *If an extra t is used,* **state** *will also be a choice.*

GA1143

Additional Phonogram Activities

Global Instructional Objective: (Fill in with each appropriate phonogram.) The learners will correctly pronounce words (or syllables) formed by adding single initial consonants, initial consonant blends, and initial consonant digraphs to the "???" phonogram.

Procedures: Several phonograms in addition to **at** and **ate** may be used in a similar fashion to the activities described above. Some phonograms to consider are **ab, ace, ack, ad, ade, ag, ail, ain, ake, all, am, ame, amp, an, and, ane, ang, ank, ap, ar, are, ark, ash, ave, ead, eak, eal, eam, ear, eat, eed, ed, eep, eet, ell, en, end, ent, est, et, ew, ice, ick, id, ide, ig, ight, ill, im, ime, in, ind, ine, ing, ink, int, ip, it, ive, ob, ock, od, og, oke, old, one, ong, oom, oon, op, ope, ore, orn, ot, ub, uff, ug, um, ump, un, ung, unk, ush,** and **ut.**

Note that this is only a partial listing of the possible phonograms which may be used with these letter cards. Any phonogram which parallels the current phonics program should be considered. Note also that words which do not follow the regular sound pattern of these phonograms may appear as the students suggest words. It is appropriate at this time to explain that letters frequently represent more than one sound. Discuss as necessary.

Additional BIG LETTER Activities

A variety of additional activities may be prepared with these cards. For example, all single letter cards may be distributed. The teacher may pronounce a word while the students scramble to form the correct spelling of that word. Note that repeated letters may be needed for this activity (for words such as **feed** or **ball**).

Consonant Blends, Consonant and Vowel Digraph Card Activities

Global Instructional Objective: The learner will identify pictorial representations of words which begin with selected initial and final consonant blends and digraphs.

Procedures: Prepare the cards on pages 32-46 as suggested with the above single letter cards. Use as suggested in the activity entitled "Single Initial Consonant Activity."

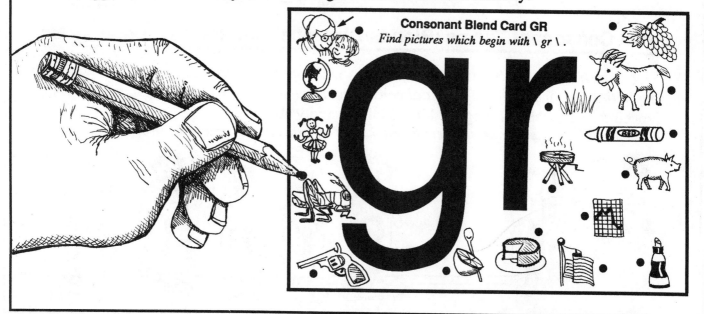

Consonant Blend Card GR
Find pictures which begin with \ gr \ .

14

Instructional Objective: Learner will accurately select words which begin with the single initial consonant sound \ d \ .

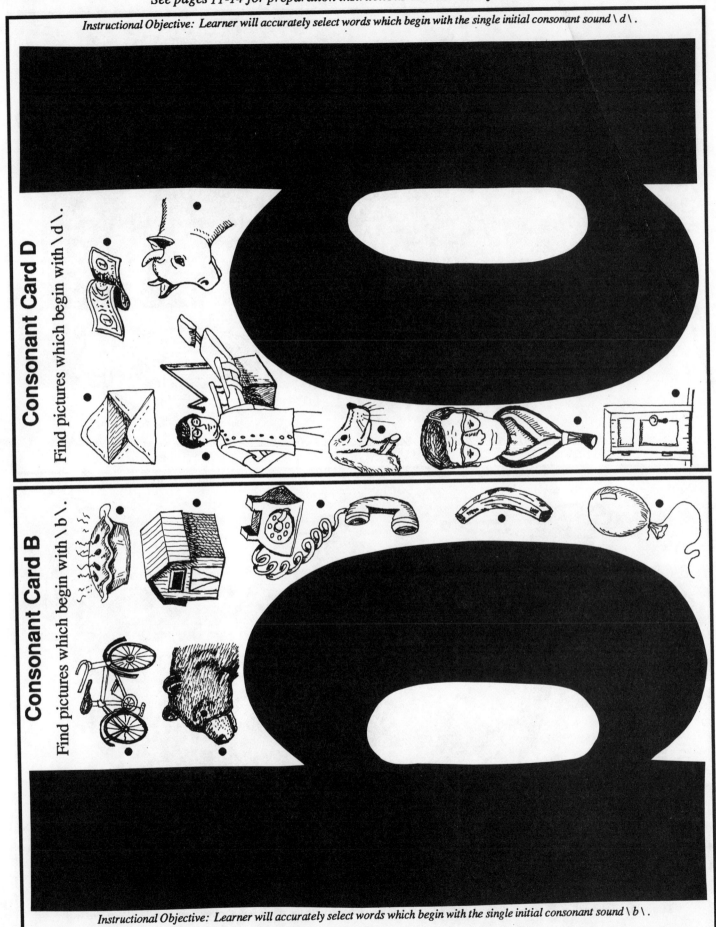

Consonant Card D
Find pictures which begin with \ d \ .

Consonant Card B
Find pictures which begin with \ b \ .

Instructional Objective: Learner will accurately select words which begin with the single initial consonant sound \ b \ .

GA1143

Consonant Card T
Find pictures which begin with \ t \.

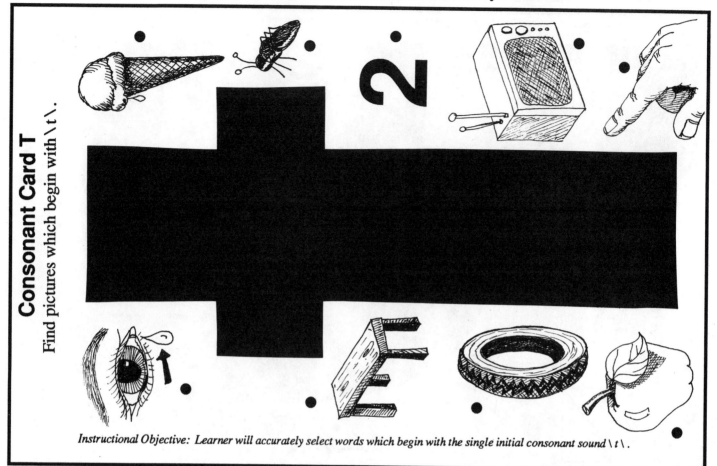

Instructional Objective: Learner will accurately select words which begin with the single initial consonant sound \ t \.

Consonant Card C
Find pictures which begin with \ k \.

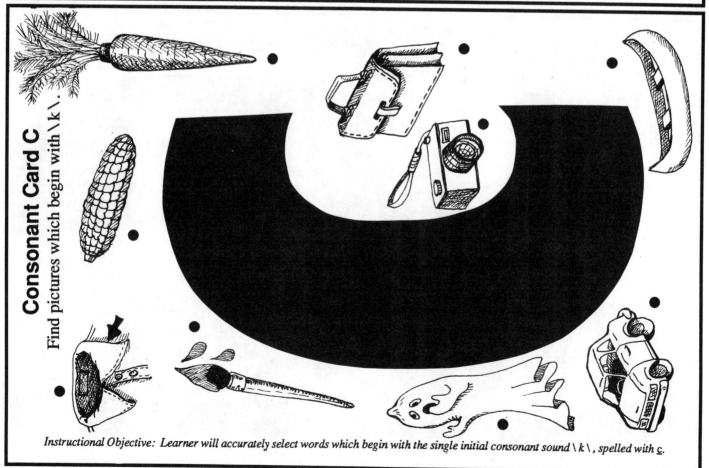

Instructional Objective: Learner will accurately select words which begin with the single initial consonant sound \ k \, spelled with c.

GA1143

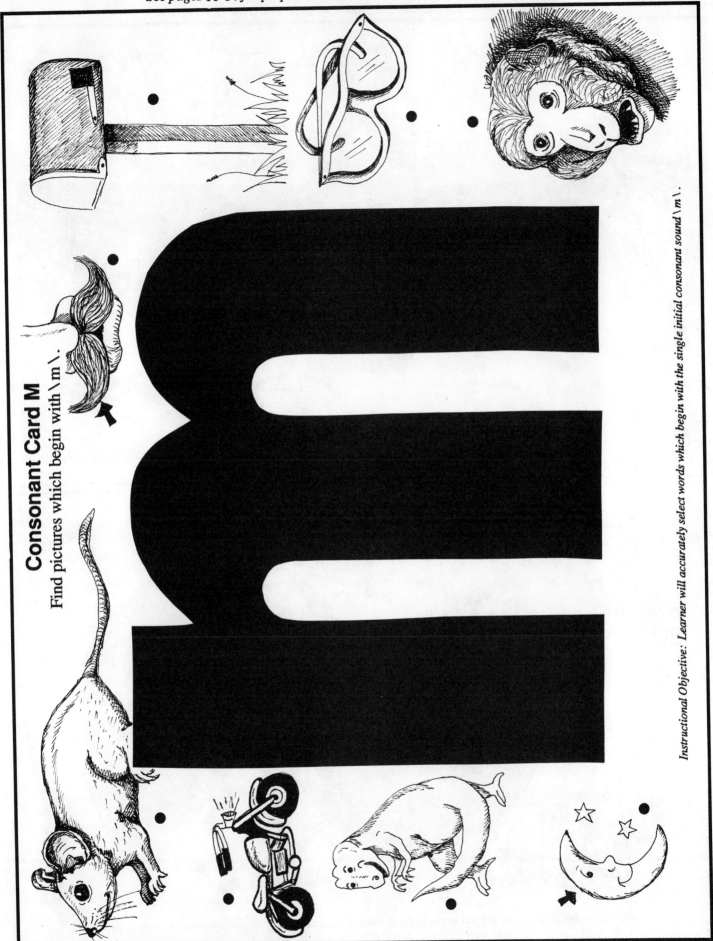

Consonant Card M
Find pictures which begin with \ m \.

Instructional Objective: Learner will accurately select words which begin with the single initial consonant sound \ m \.

GA1143

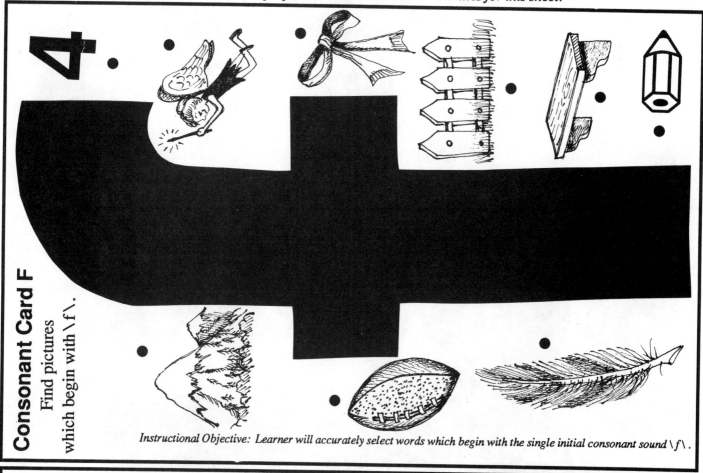

Consonant Card F
Find pictures which begin with \ f \.

Instructional Objective: Learner will accurately select words which begin with the single initial consonant sound \ f \.

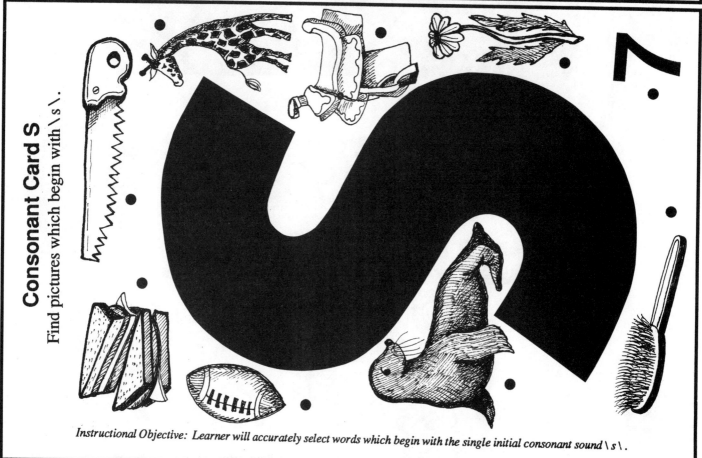

Consonant Card S
Find pictures which begin with \ s \.

Instructional Objective: Learner will accurately select words which begin with the single initial consonant sound \ s \.

GA1143

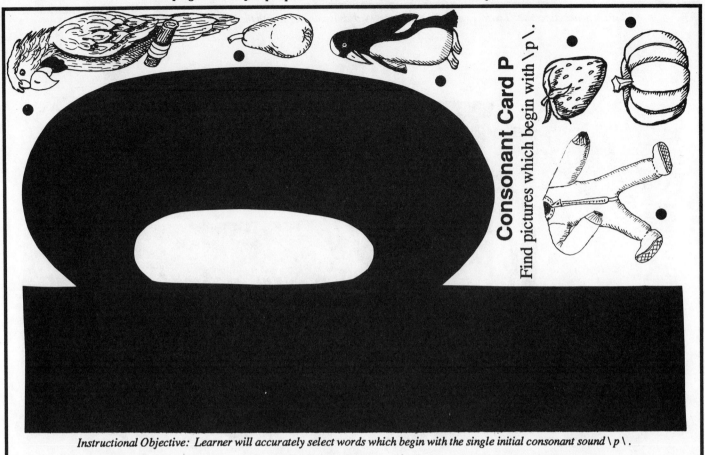

Consonant Card P

Find pictures which begin with \ p \.

Instructional Objective: Learner will accurately select words which begin with the single initial consonant sound \ p \.

Instructional Objective: Learner will accurately select words which begin with the single initial consonant sound \ g \.

Consonant Card G

Find pictures which begin with \ g \.

GA1143

Instructional Objective: Learner will accurately select words which begin with the single initial consonant sound \ r \ .

Consonant Card R
Find pictures which begin with \ r \ .

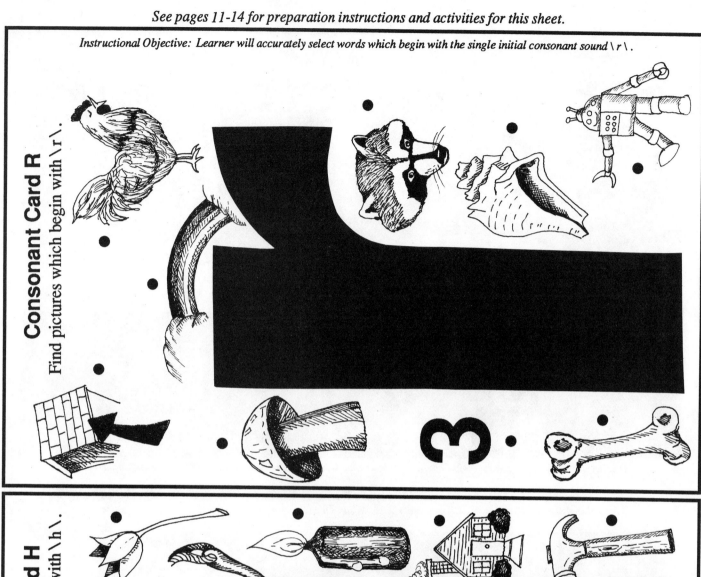

Consonant Card H
Find pictures which begin with \ h \ .

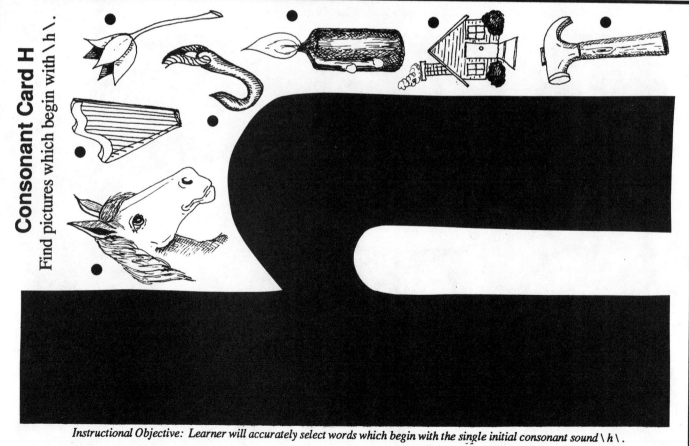

Instructional Objective: Learner will accurately select words which begin with the single initial consonant sound \ h \ .

20

GA1143

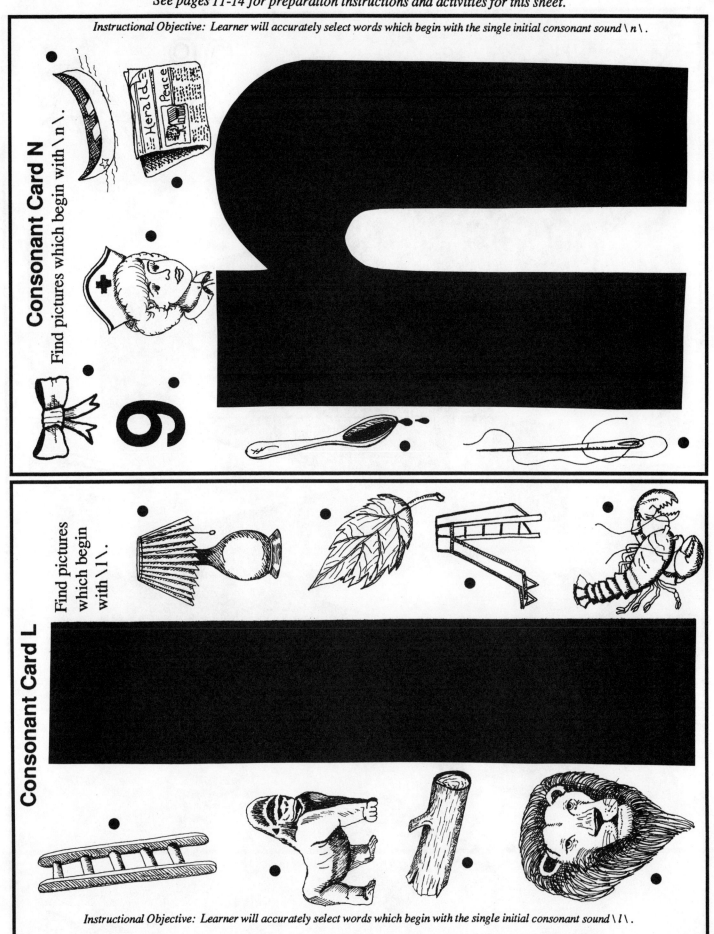

Instructional Objective: Learner will accurately select words which begin with the single initial consonant sound \ n \ .

Consonant Card N

Find pictures which begin with \ n \ .

Consonant Card L

Find pictures which begin with \ l \ .

Instructional Objective: Learner will accurately select words which begin with the single initial consonant sound \ l \ .

21

GA1143

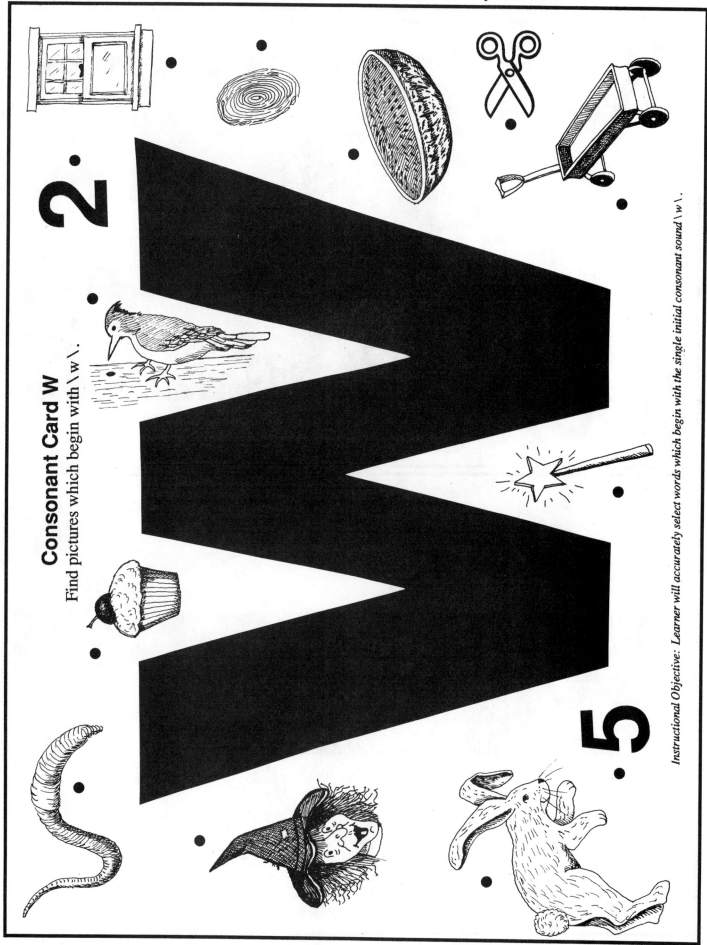

Consonant Card W
Find pictures which begin with \w\.

Instructional Objective: Learner will accurately select words which begin with the single initial consonant sound \w\.

22

GA1143

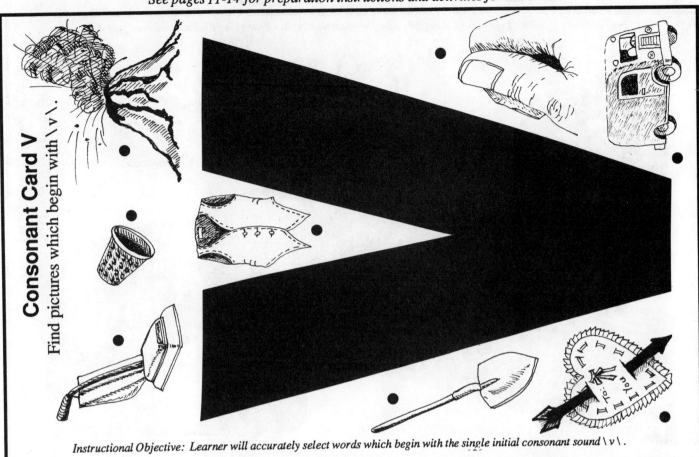

Consonant Card V
Find pictures which begin with \ v \.

Instructional Objective: Learner will accurately select words which begin with the single initial consonant sound \ v \.

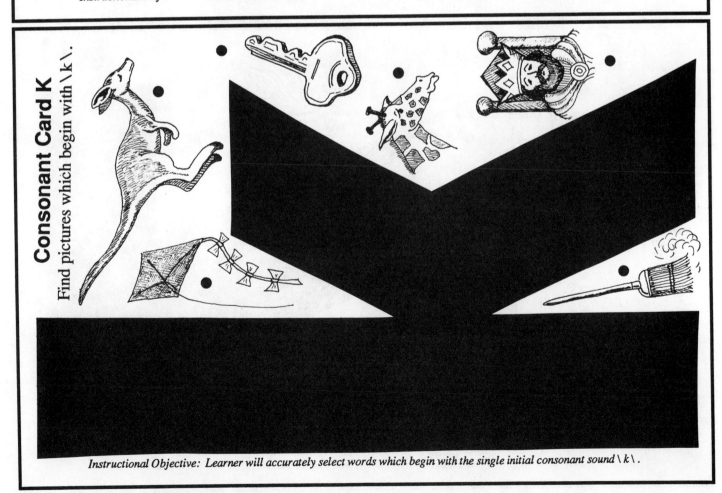

Consonant Card K
Find pictures which begin with \ k \.

Instructional Objective: Learner will accurately select words which begin with the single initial consonant sound \ k \.

23

GA1143

See pages 11-14 for preparation instructions and activities for this sheet.

Instructional Objective: Learner will accurately select words which begin with the single initial consonant sound \ y \ .

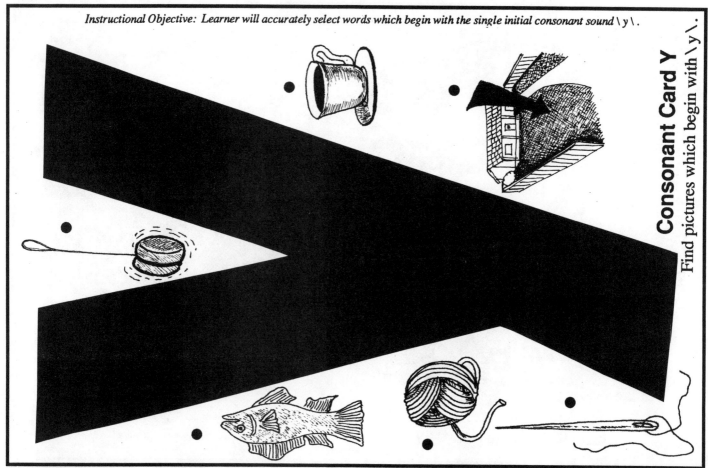

Consonant Card Y
Find pictures which begin with \ y \ .

Consonant Card Z
Find pictures which begin with \ z \ .

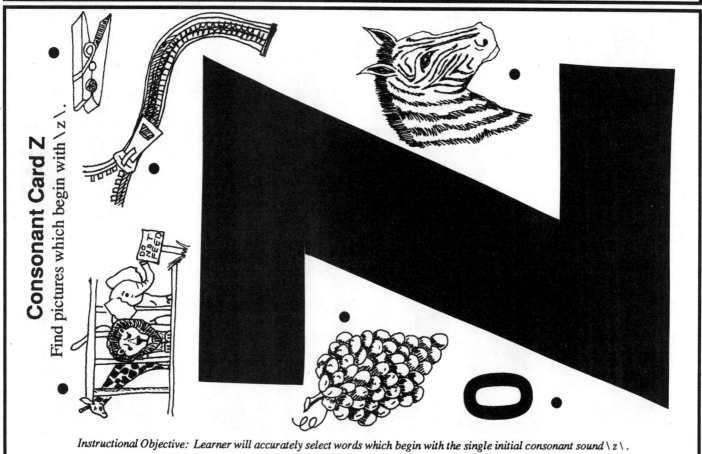

Instructional Objective: Learner will accurately select words which begin with the single initial consonant sound \ z \ .

GA1143

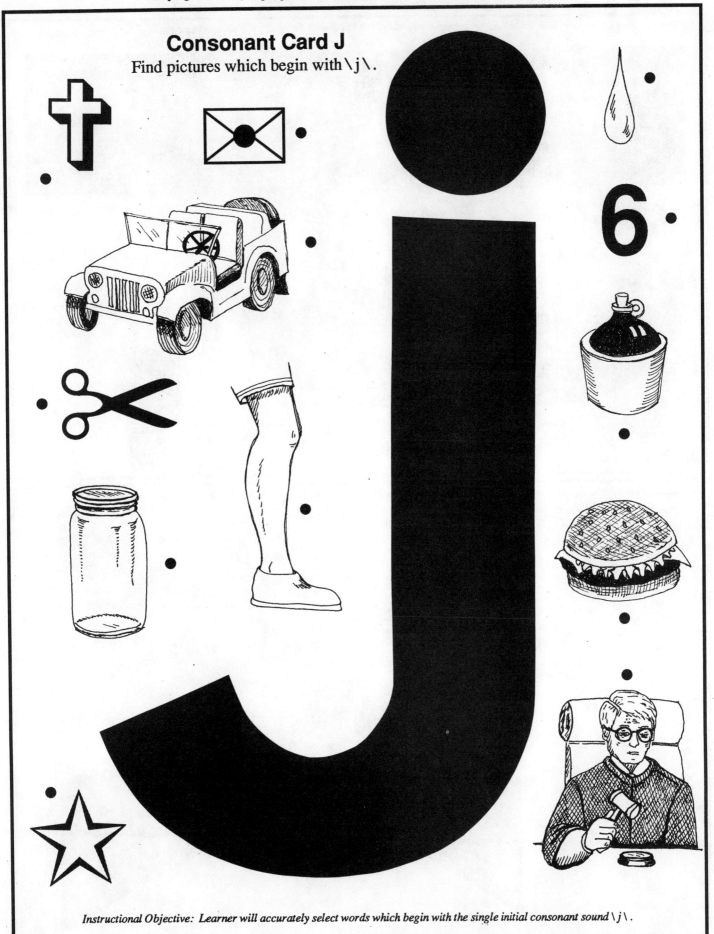

Consonant Card J
Find pictures which begin with \ j \ .

Instructional Objective: Learner will accurately select words which begin with the single initial consonant sound \ j \ .

Copyright © 1990, Good Apple, Inc.

25

GA1144

Instructional Objective: Learner will accurately select words which begin with the single initial consonant sounds \ kw \ , spelled with q.

Consonant Card Q
Find pictures which begin with \ kw \ .

Instructional Objective: Learner will accurately select words which begin with the single initial consonant sound \ z \ , spelled with x.

Consonant Card X
Find pictures which begin with \ z \ .

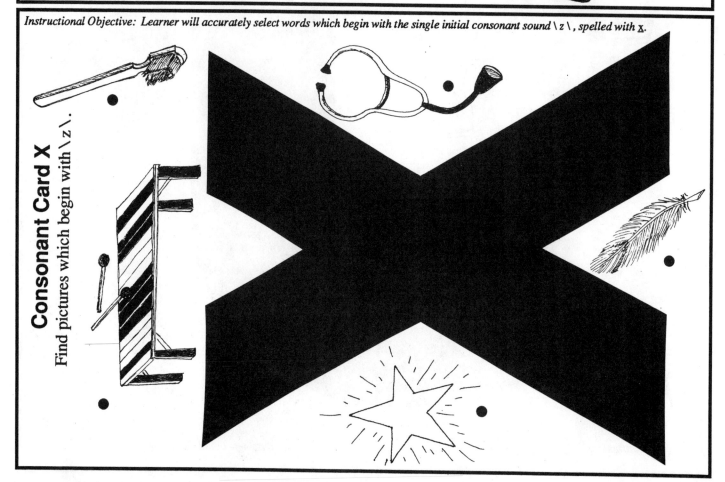

GA1143

See pages 11-14 for preparation instructions and activities for this sheet.

Instructional Objective: Learner will accurately select words which contain the short a vowel sound.

Short A Vowel Card
Find pictures with the short a vowel sound.

Instructional Objective: Learner will accurately select words which contain the long a vowel sound.

Long A Vowel Card
Find pictures with the long a vowel sound.

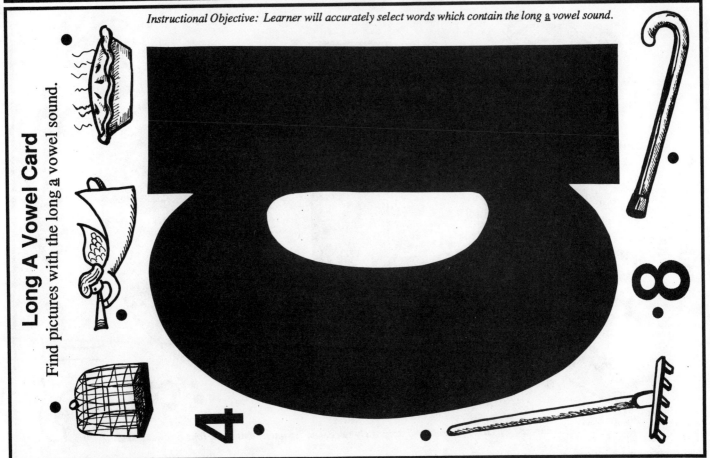

27

GA1143

Short E Vowel Card
Find pictures with the short e vowel sound.

Instructional Objective: Learner will accurately select words which contain the short e vowel sound.

Long E Vowel Card
Find pictures with the long e vowel sound.

Instructional Objective: Learner will accurately select words which contain the long e vowel sound.

GA1143

Short I Vowel Card

Find pictures with the short i vowel sound.

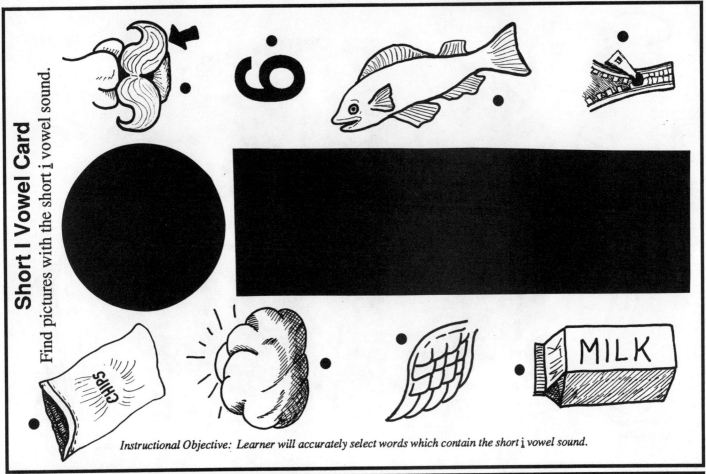

Instructional Objective: Learner will accurately select words which contain the short i̧ vowel sound.

Long I Vowel Card

Find pictures with the long i vowel sound.

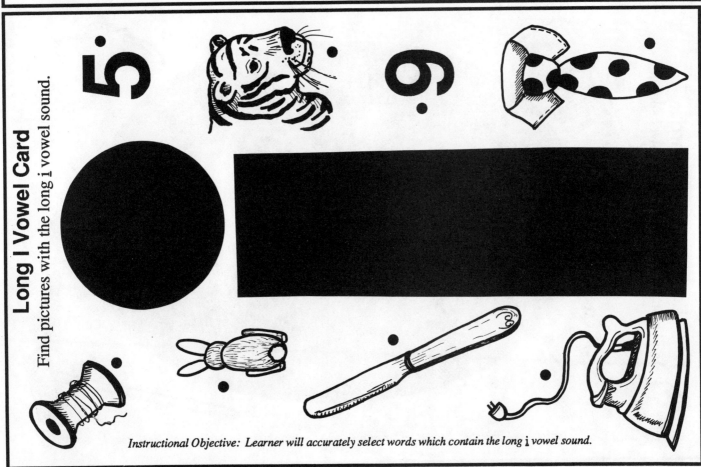

Instructional Objective: Learner will accurately select words which contain the long i̧ vowel sound.

GA1143

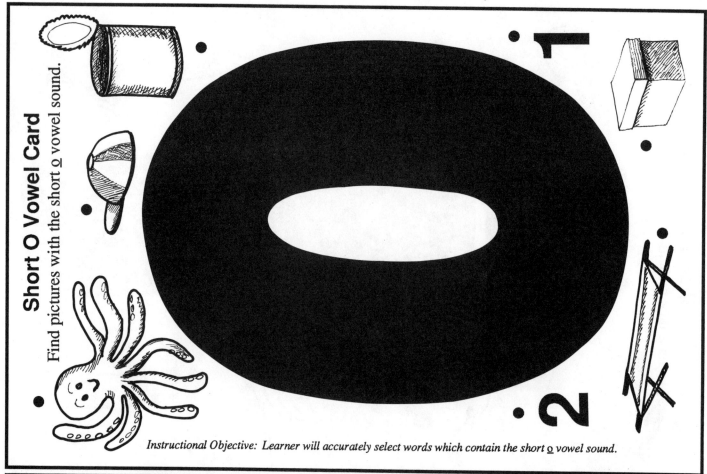

Short O Vowel Card
Find pictures with the short o vowel sound.

Instructional Objective: Learner will accurately select words which contain the short o vowel sound.

Long O Vowel Card
Find pictures with the long o vowel sound.

Instructional Objective: Learner will accurately select words which contain the long o vowel sound.

GA1143

Instructional Objective: Learner will accurately select words which contain the short u̲ vowel sound.

Short U Vowel Card
Find pictures with the short u̲ vowel sound.

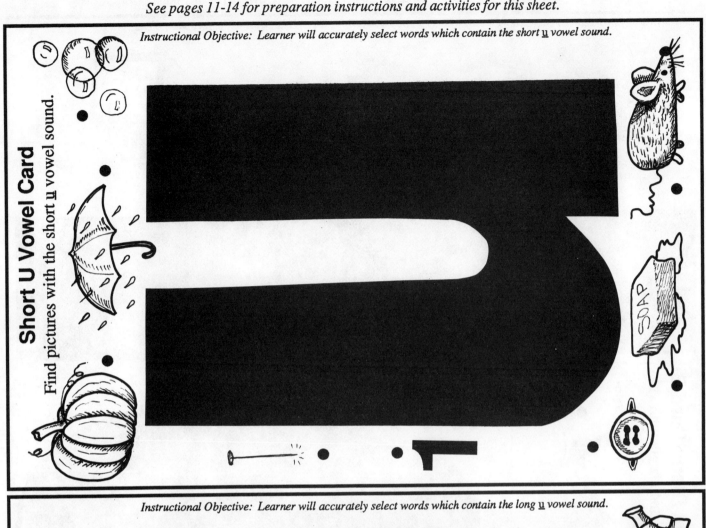

Instructional Objective: Learner will accurately select words which contain the long u̲ vowel sound.

Long U Vowel Card
Find pictures with the long u̲ vowel sound.

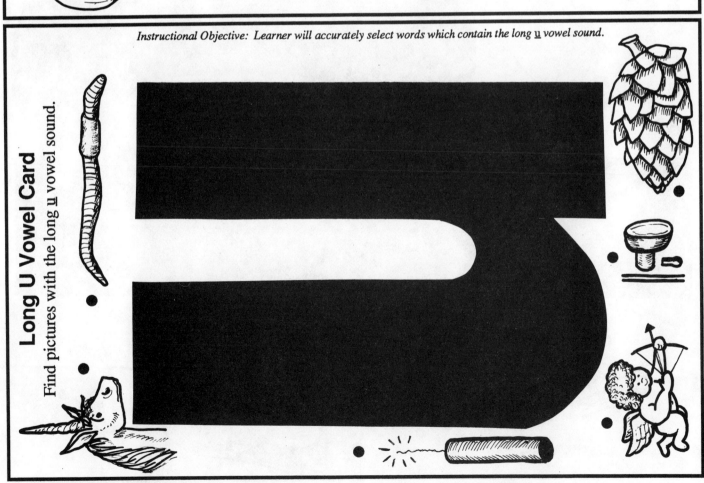

31

GA1143

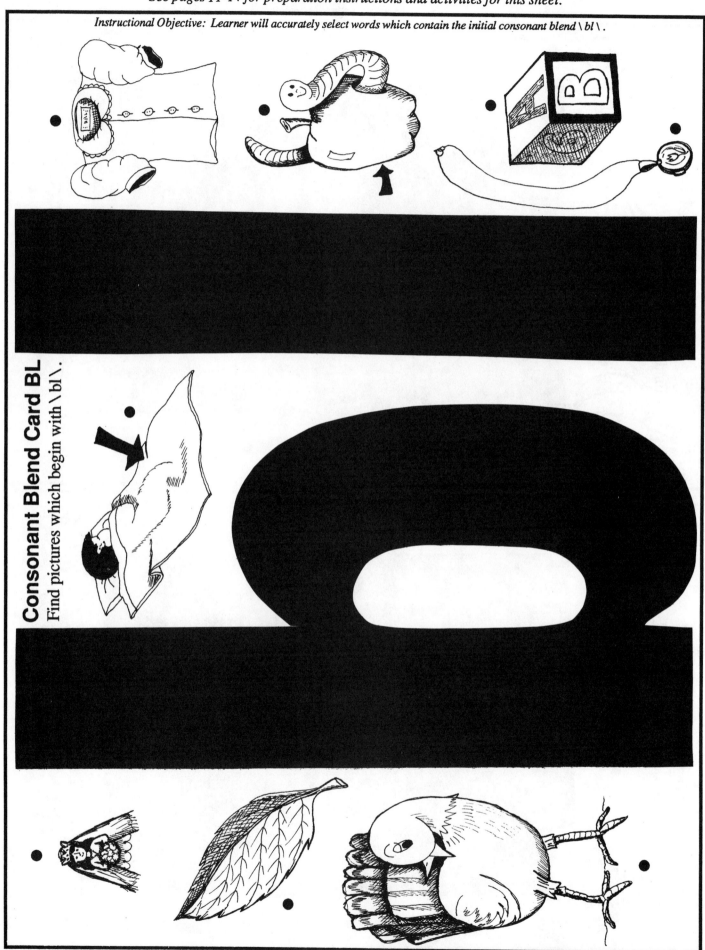

Instructional Objective: Learner will accurately select words which contain the initial consonant blend \ bl \ .

Consonant Blend Card BL
Find pictures which begin with \ bl \ .

32

GA1143

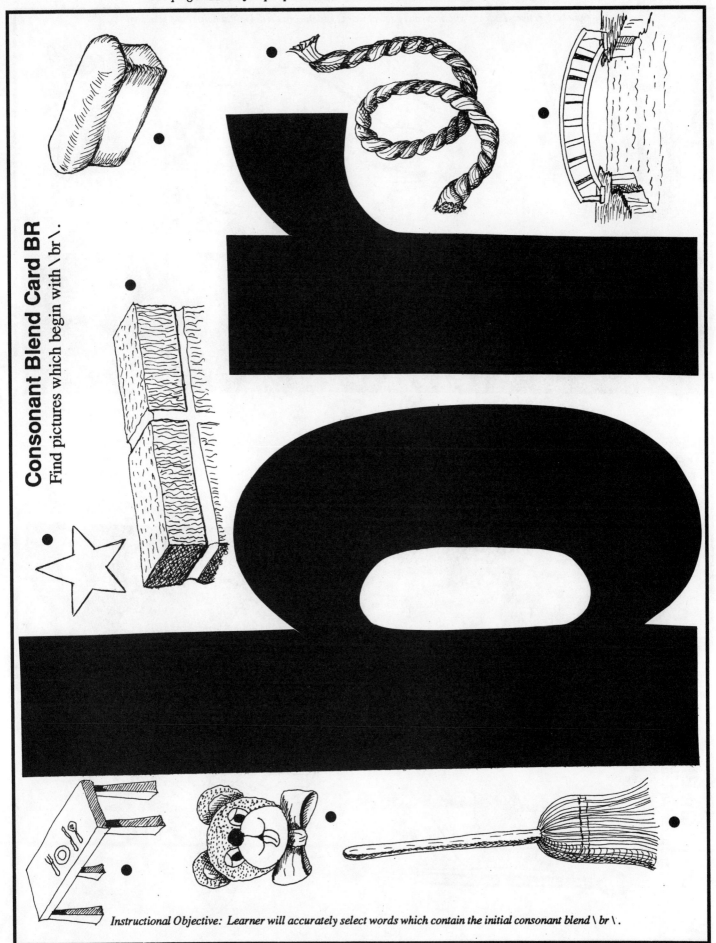

Consonant Blend Card BR
Find pictures which begin with \ br \.

Instructional Objective: Learner will accurately select words which contain the initial consonant blend \ br \.

GA1143

Instructional Objective: Learner will accurately select words which contain the initial consonant blend \fl\ .

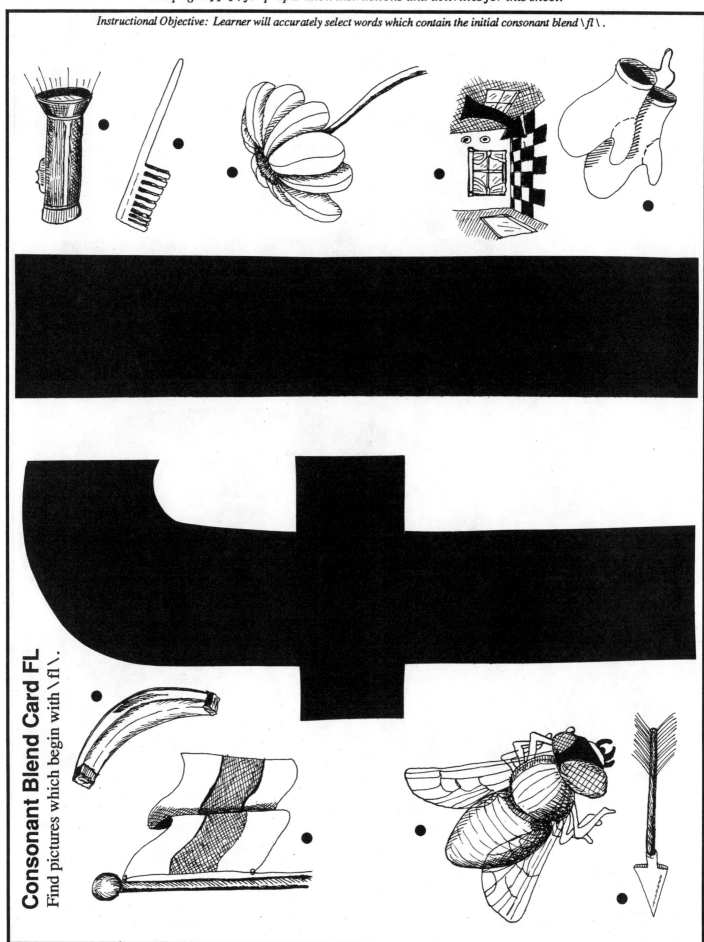

Consonant Blend Card FL
Find pictures which begin with \fl\.

Consonant Blend Card SN

Find pictures which begin with \ sn \.

Instructional Objective: Learner will accurately select words which contain the initial consonant blend \ sn \.

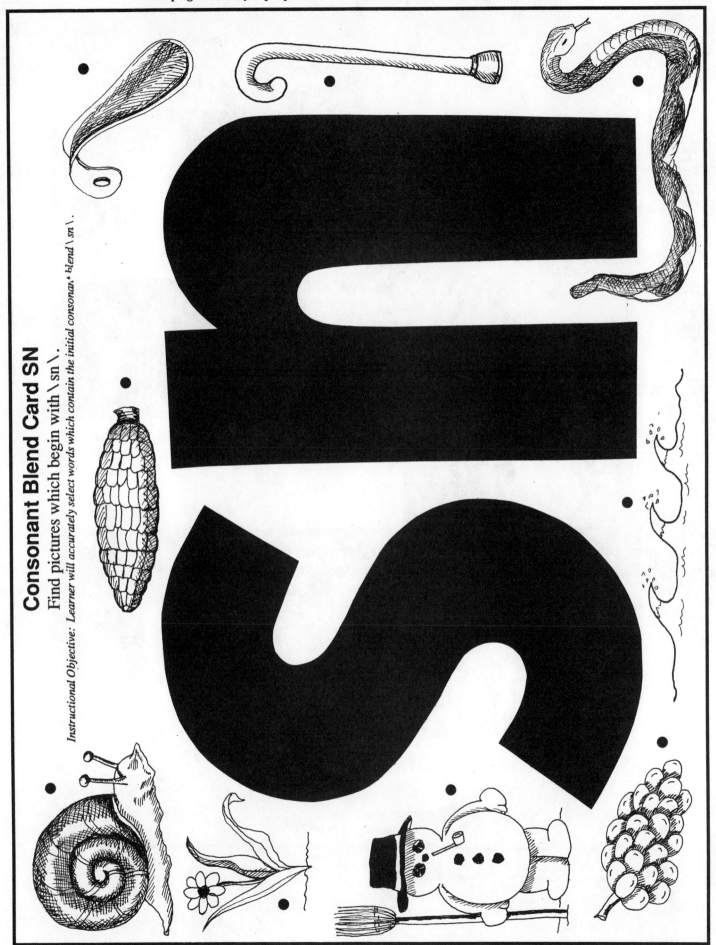

GA1143

Consonant Blend Card TR

Find pictures which begin with \ tr \.

Instructional Objective: Learner will accurately select words which contain the initial consonant blend \ tr \.

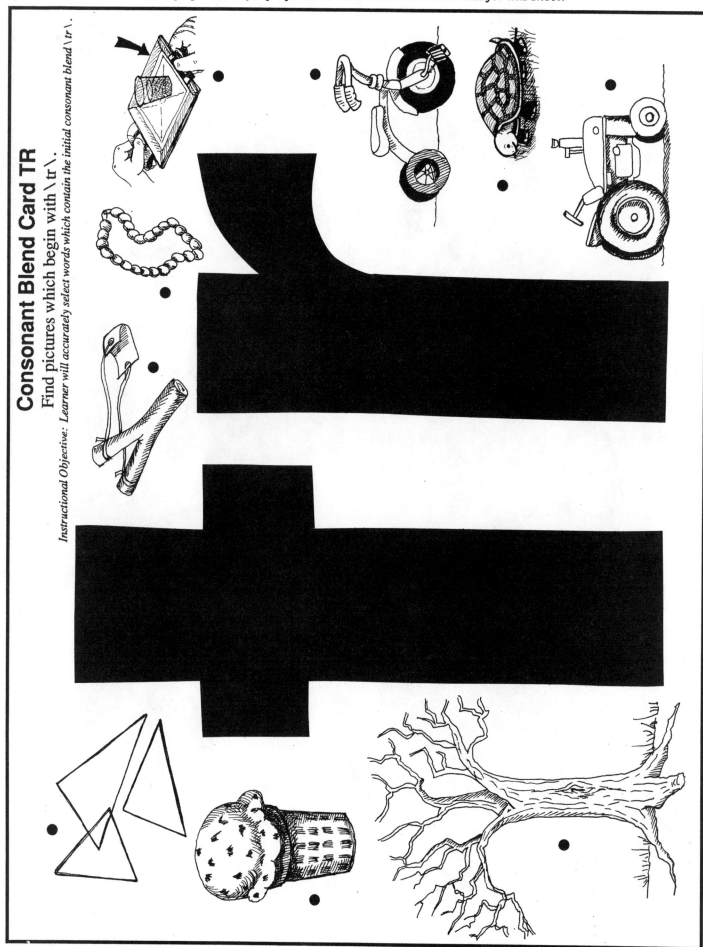

GA1143

Consonant Blend Card GR

Find pictures which begin with \ gr \.

Instructional Objective: Learner will accurately select words which begin with the initial consonant blend \ gr \.

GA1143

See pages 11-14 for preparation instructions and activities for this sheet.

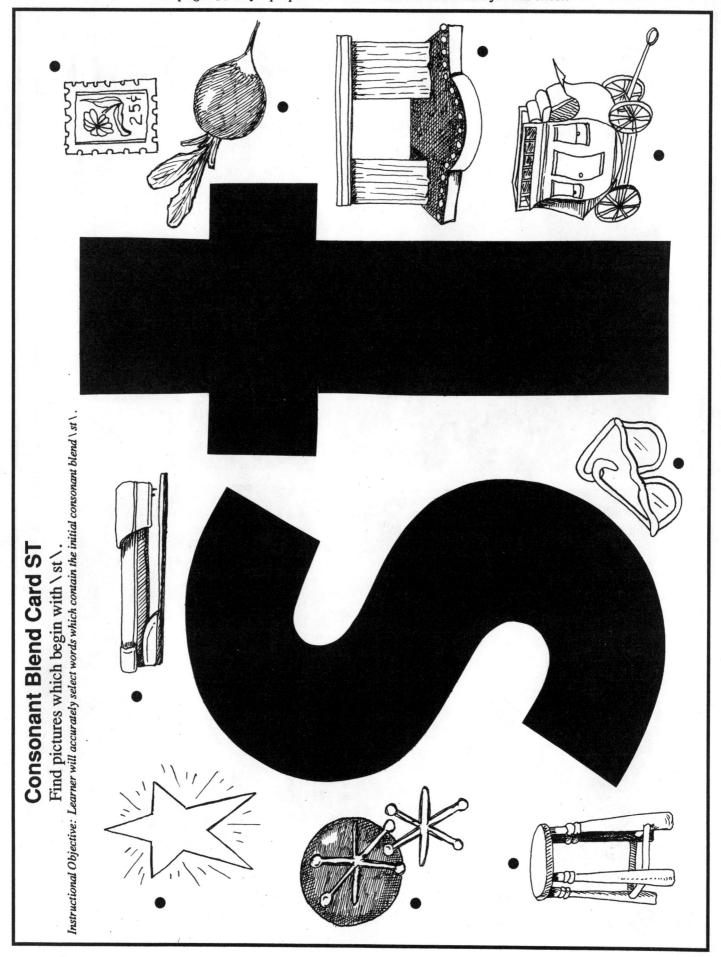

Consonant Blend Card ST
Find pictures which begin with \ st \.

Instructional Objective: Learner will accurately select words which contain the initial consonant blend \ st \.

Copyright © 1990, Good Apple, Inc.

38

GA1143

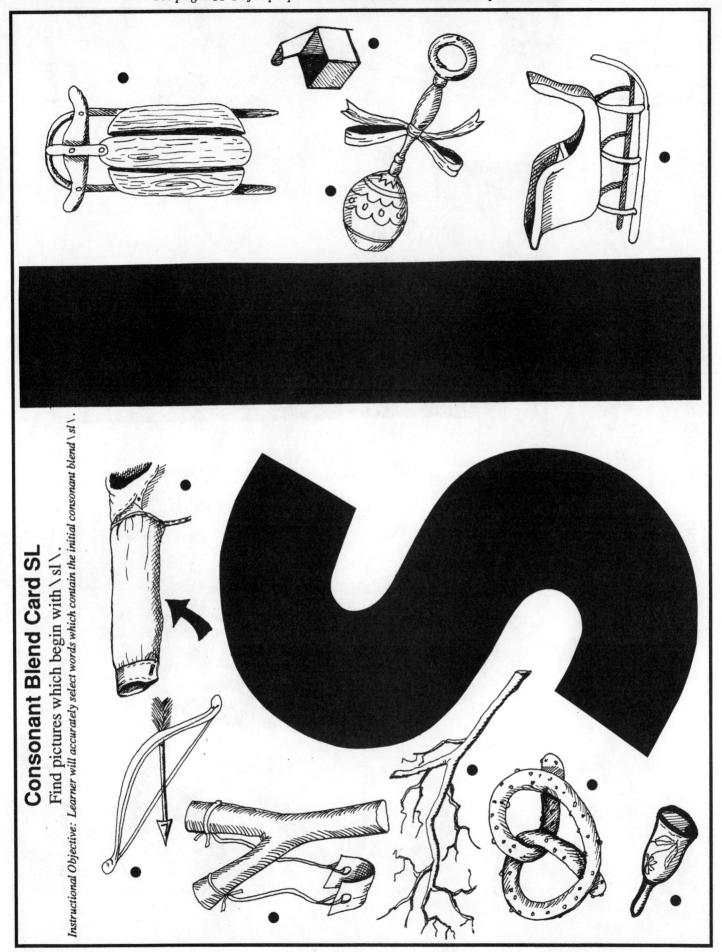

Consonant Blend Card SL

Find pictures which begin with \ sl \.

Instructional Objective: Learner will accurately select words which contain the initial consonant blend \ sl \.

GA1143

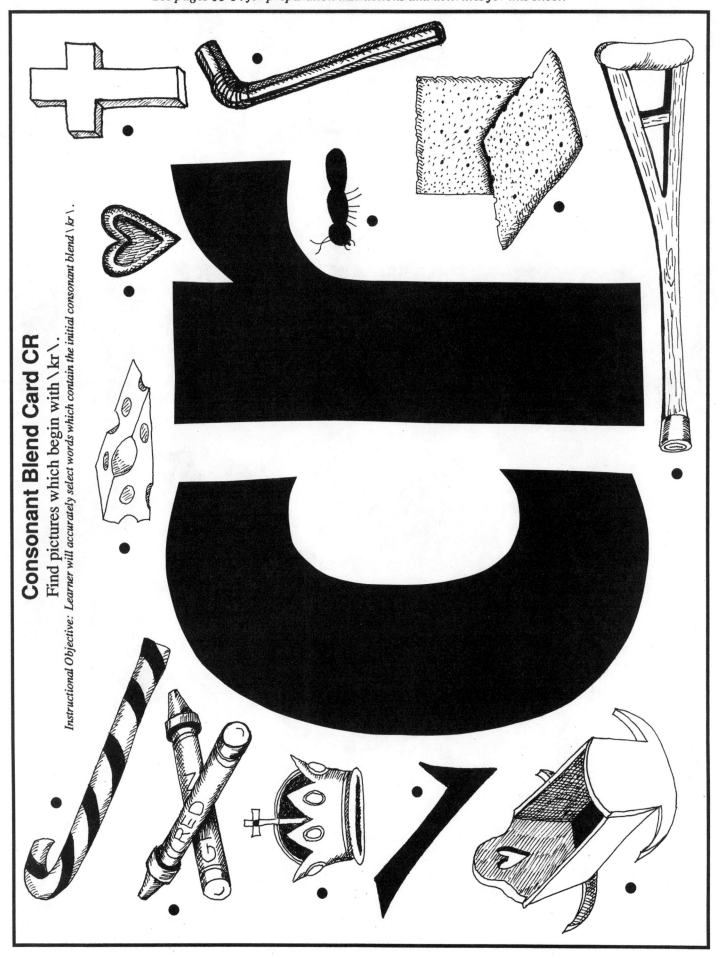

Consonant Blend Card CR

Find pictures which begin with \ kr \.

Instructional Objective: Learner will accurately select words which contain the initial consonant blend \ kr \.

GA1143

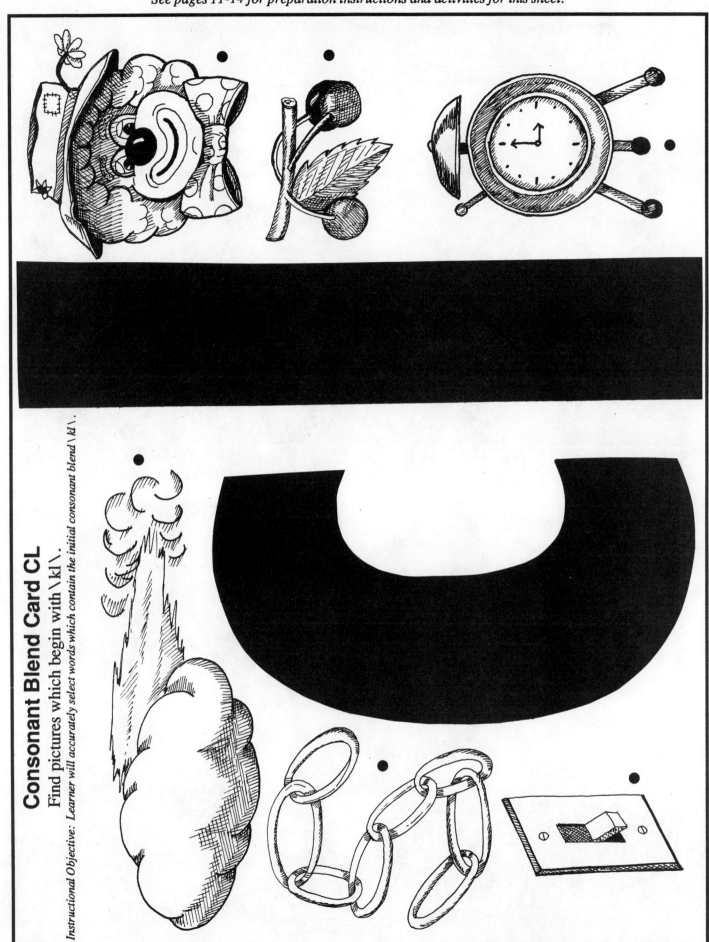

Consonant Blend Card CL

Find pictures which begin with \kl\.

Instructional Objective: Learner will accurately select words which contain the initial consonant blend \kl\.

GA1143

See pages 11-14 for preparation instructions and activities for this sheet.

Instructional Objective: Learner will accurately select words which contain the initial consonant blend \ sk \ .

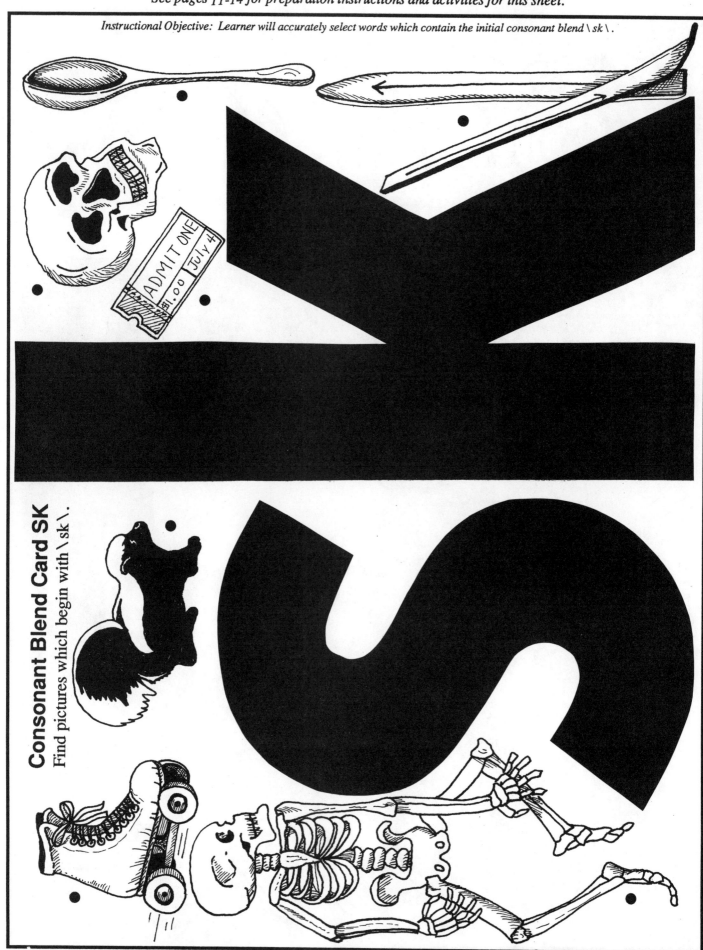

Consonant Blend Card SK
Find pictures which begin with \ sk \ .

42

GA1143

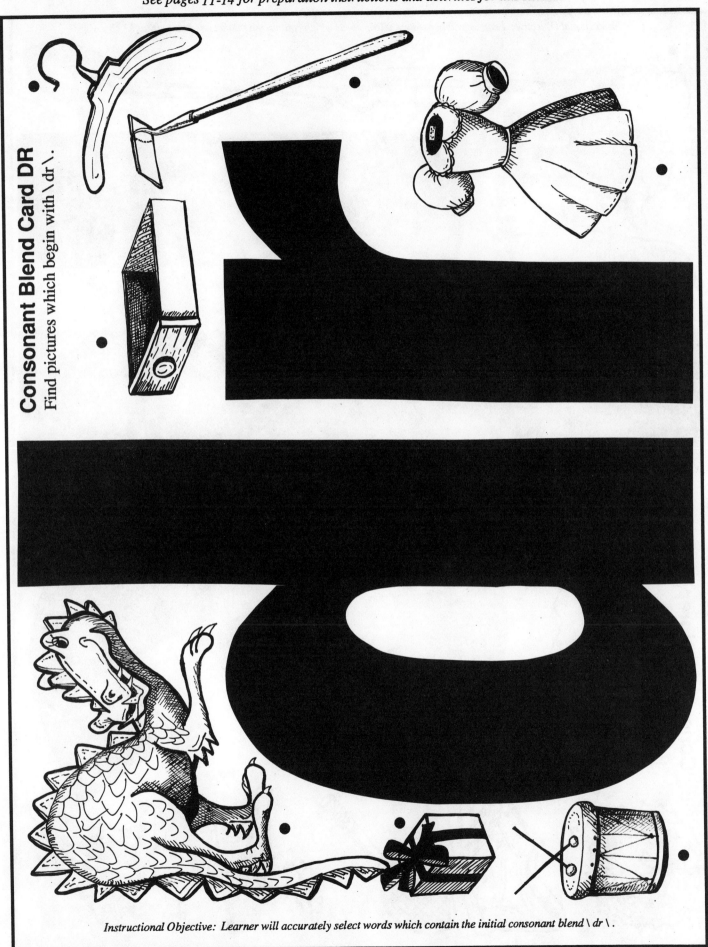

Consonant Blend Card DR
Find pictures which begin with \ dr \.

Instructional Objective: Learner will accurately select words which contain the initial consonant blend \ dr \.

GA1143

Instructional Objective: Learner will accurately select words which contain the initial consonant digraph \ sh \ .

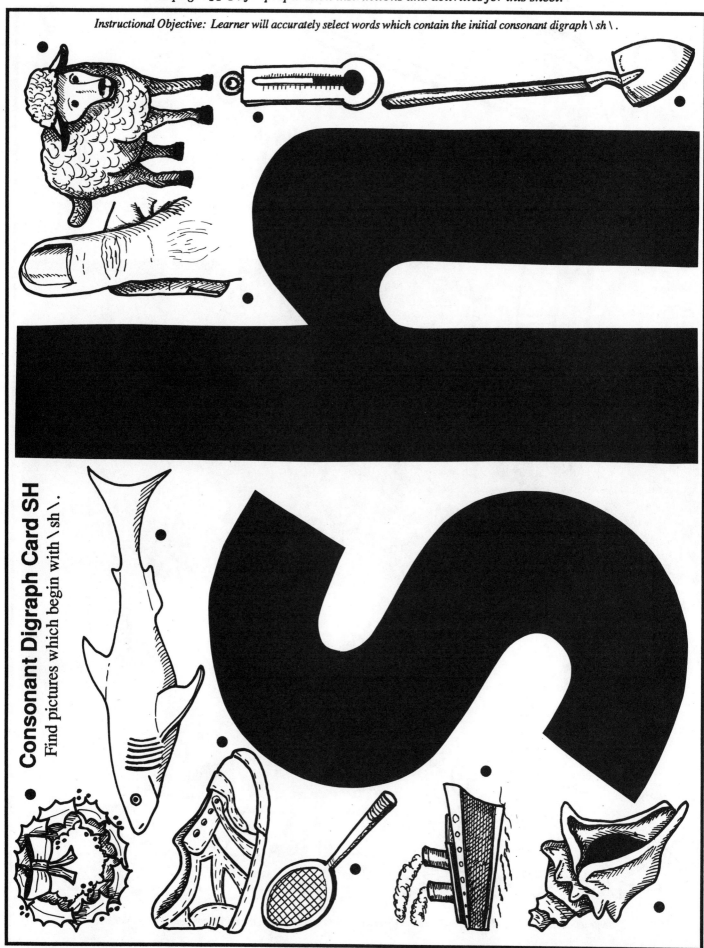

Consonant Digraph Card SH
Find pictures which begin with \ sh \.

GA1143

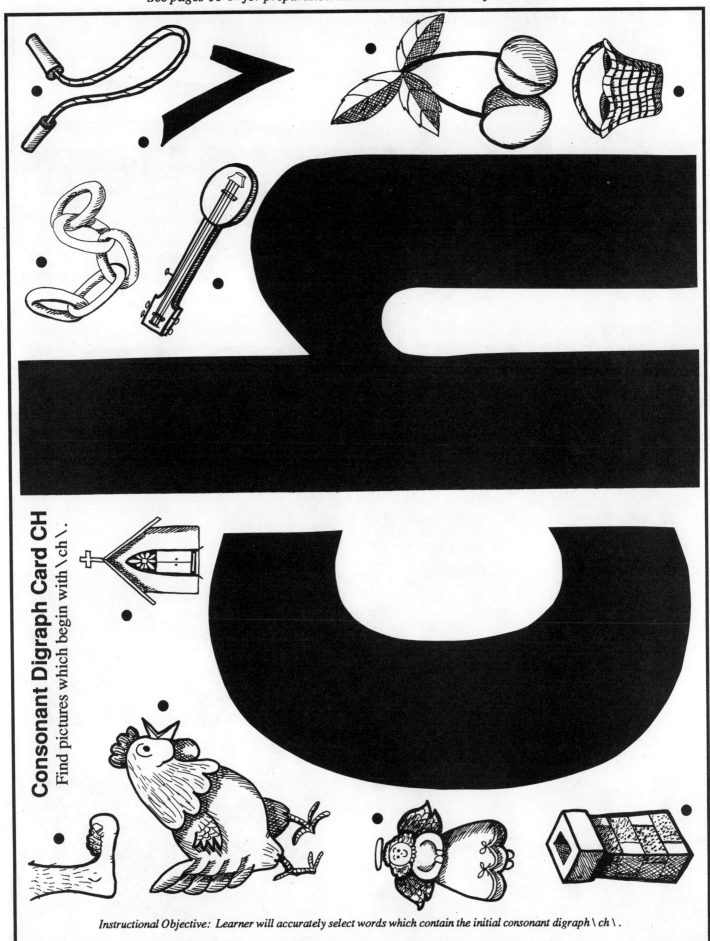

Consonant Digraph Card CH
Find pictures which begin with \ ch \ .

Instructional Objective: Learner will accurately select words which contain the initial consonant digraph \ ch \ .

GA1143

Instructional Objective: Learner will accurately select words which contain the initial consonant digraph \ th \.

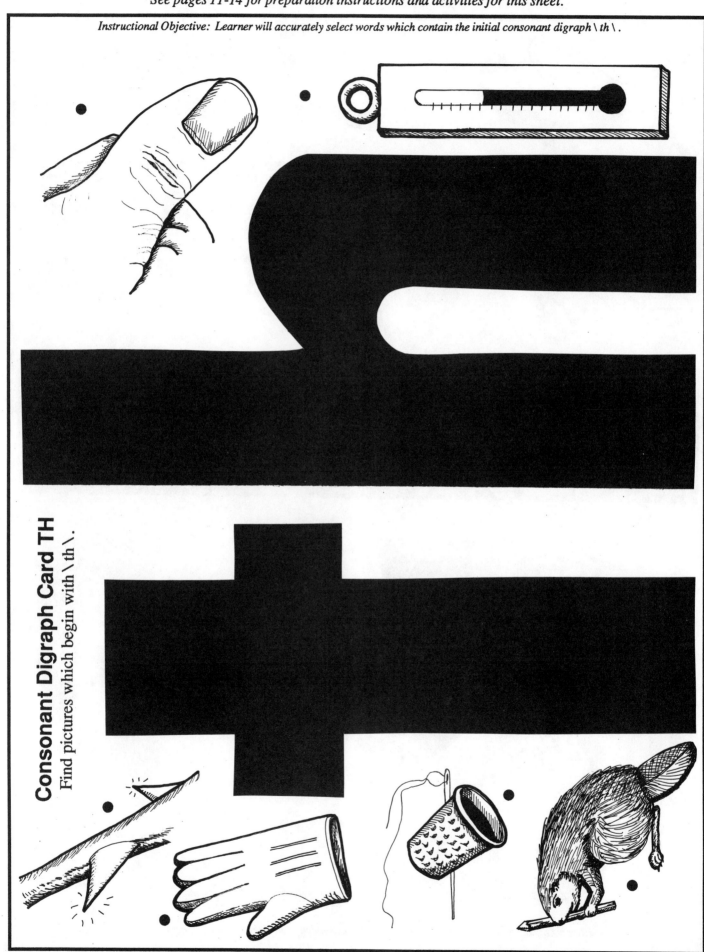

Consonant Digraph Card TH
Find pictures which begin with \ th \.

46

GA1143

SECTION 3

PHONICS TASK CARDS

Many types of task cards exist for teaching the basic subskills of phonics. The cards shown on pages 49-64 may be prepared for teaching the adding of initial consonant elements to frequently used phonograms.

Preparation: The provided phonics task cards may be photocopied from this text and mounted onto large colorful sheets of heavy paper. They may also be traced or drawn onto heavy paper. For each card cut a long strip of matching heavy paper which is approximately two inches in width and at least a foot in length. (Some cards will need longer strips.) On one side of these strips write the initial single consonant letters and on the other side write the initial consonant teams (suggested below). Slit the patterns at the dotted lines and insert the prepared strips. For photocopies pasted onto heavy paper, a strip of double-stick tape should be placed at the dotted lines **in between** the photocopy and the support paper.

Student Use: One card should be used to explain to the entire group how the strips slide through the designs in order to form new words. Students should be instructed to try to pronounce the name of the shape in order to determine the pronunciation of the phonogram used. Note that some of the suggested consonants/teams listed below may be omitted for very young learners. The strip should be inserted with the single letters showing for the beginning readers. As the readers mature, the side with the consonant teams may be used. Learners should be encouraged to pronounce all of the words, even the ones with which they are unfamiliar.

Instructional Objective: The learner will determine the pronunciation of new words by voicing an indicated phonogram then adding a variety of initial single consonant sounds (letters) or consonant teams (blends or digraphs).

Suggested Letters for Strips: The following are suggestions for letters or to be placed on the strips for the provided designs. Modify as needed or desired. Note that the semicolon separates the letters which should appear on different sides.

pig: *b, d, f, g, j, p, r, w, z; br, spr, sw, tr, tw*
cat: *b, c, f, h, m, p, r, s, t, v; br, ch, dr, fl, gn, sc, sl, sp, spl, th*
cow: *b, c, h, n, p, r, s, v, w; br, pl, ch, pr, sc*
can: *b, c, D, f, J, m, N, p, r, t, v; br, cl, fl, pl, sc, sp, th*
cap: *c, g, l, m, n, r, s, t, z; ch, cl, fl, sl, scr, sn, str, tr, wr*
saw: *c, j, l, p, r, s; cl, cr, dr, fl, gn, sl, str, squ*
bag: *b, g, h, j, l, n, r, s, t, w, z; br, cr, dr, fl, sh, sl, sn, st, sw*
bed: *b, f, l, N, r, T, w; bl, br, fl, Fr, sh, shr, sl, sp*
top: *b, c, h, m, p, s, t; ch, cr, dr, fl, pl, pr, sh, sl, st*
bell: *b, c, d, f, j, N, s, t, w, y; dw, qu, sh, sm, sp, sw*
star: *b, c, f, j, m, p, t; ch, sc, sp, st*
tree: *b, f, D, g, l, s, t, w; fl, fr, gl, gr, kn, spr, th, tr, thr, wh*
sock: *d, h, l, m, r, s, t; bl, ch, cl, cr, fl, fr, kn, sh, sm, st*
book: *b, c, h, l, n, r, t; br, cr, sh*
boot: *b, h, l, m, r, t; sc, sh*
nine: *d, f, l, m, n, p, t, v, w; br, sh, shr, sp, sw, wh*

How now?

-OW

GA1143

After students use these shapes, they may draw and prepare additional ones. The following shows a sample prepared phonics task card (reduced in size):

48

GA1143

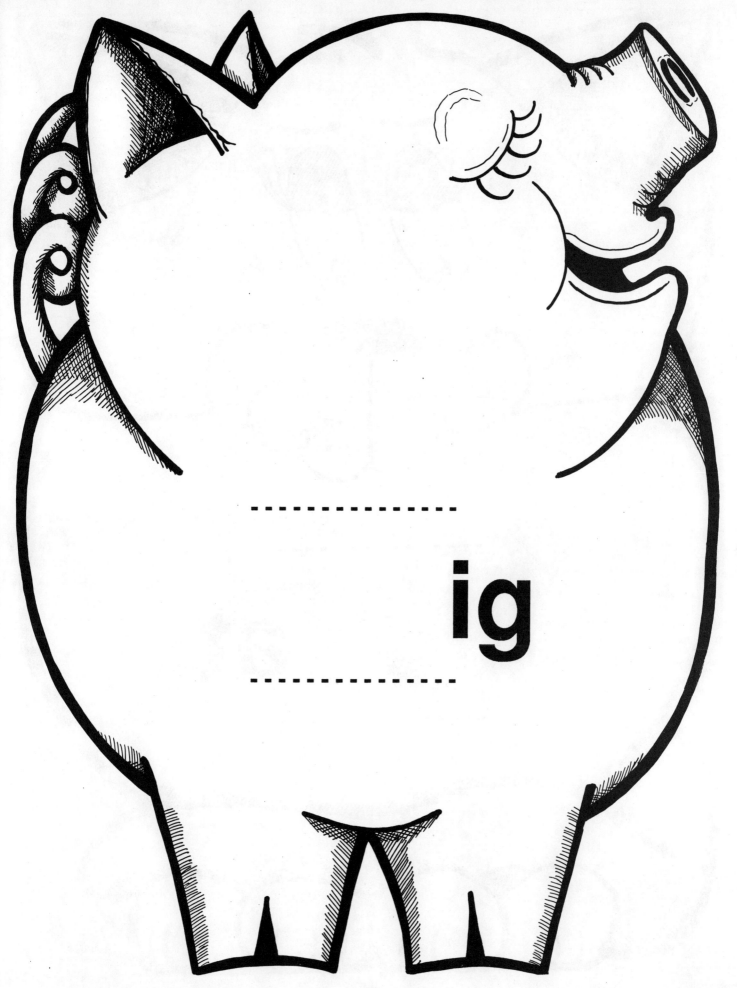

ig

GA1143

at

50

GA1143

OW

51

an

GA1143

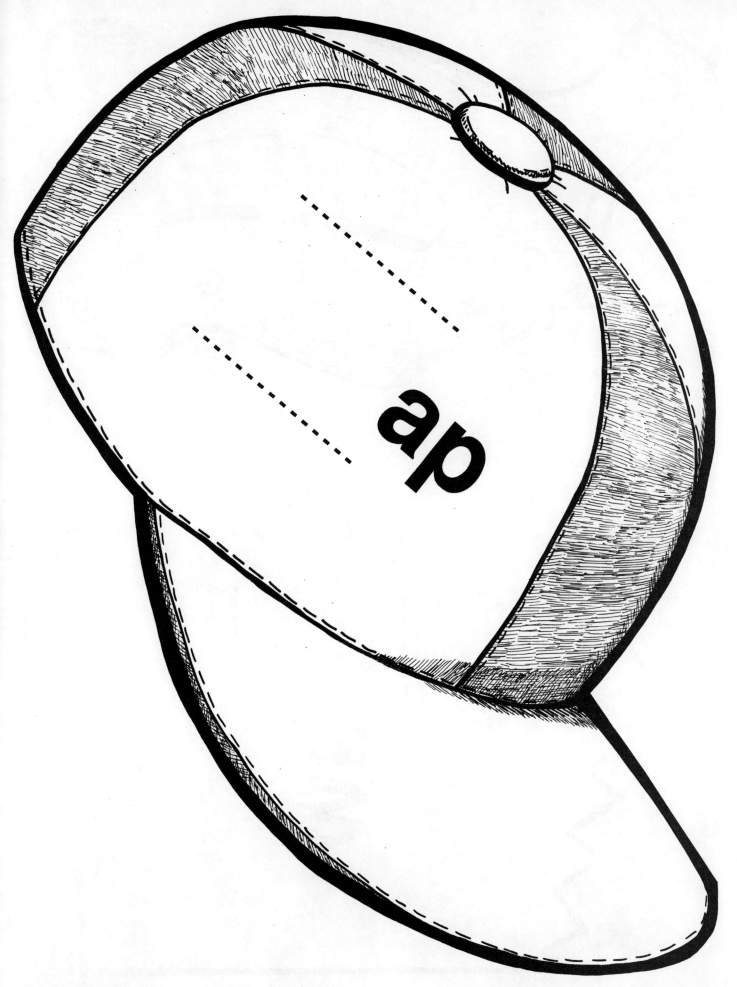

GA1143

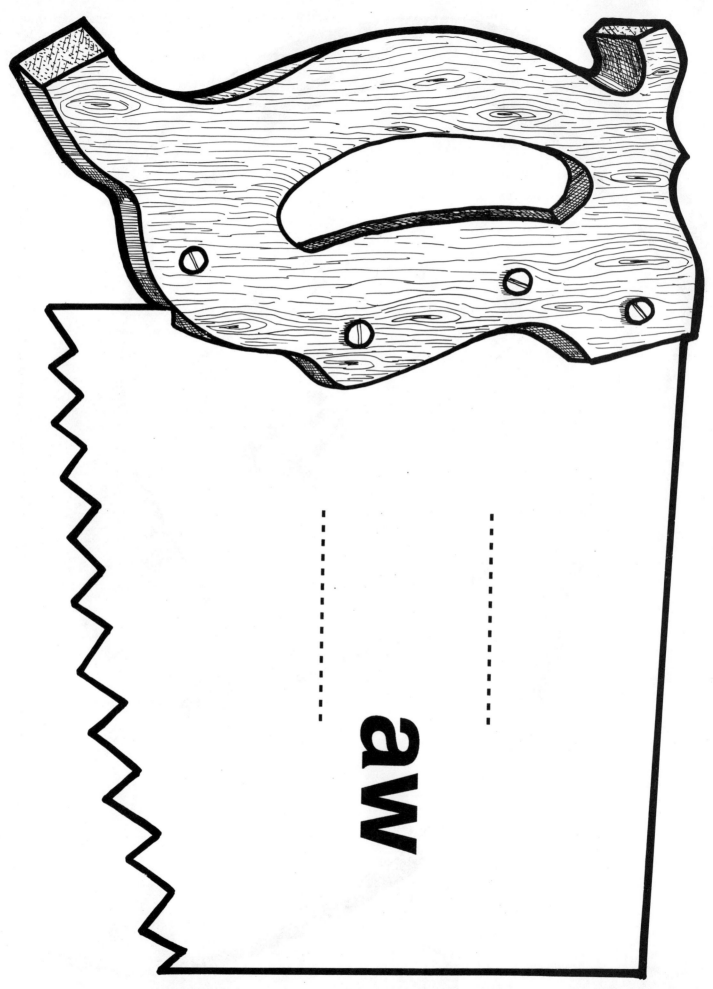

aw

54

GA1143

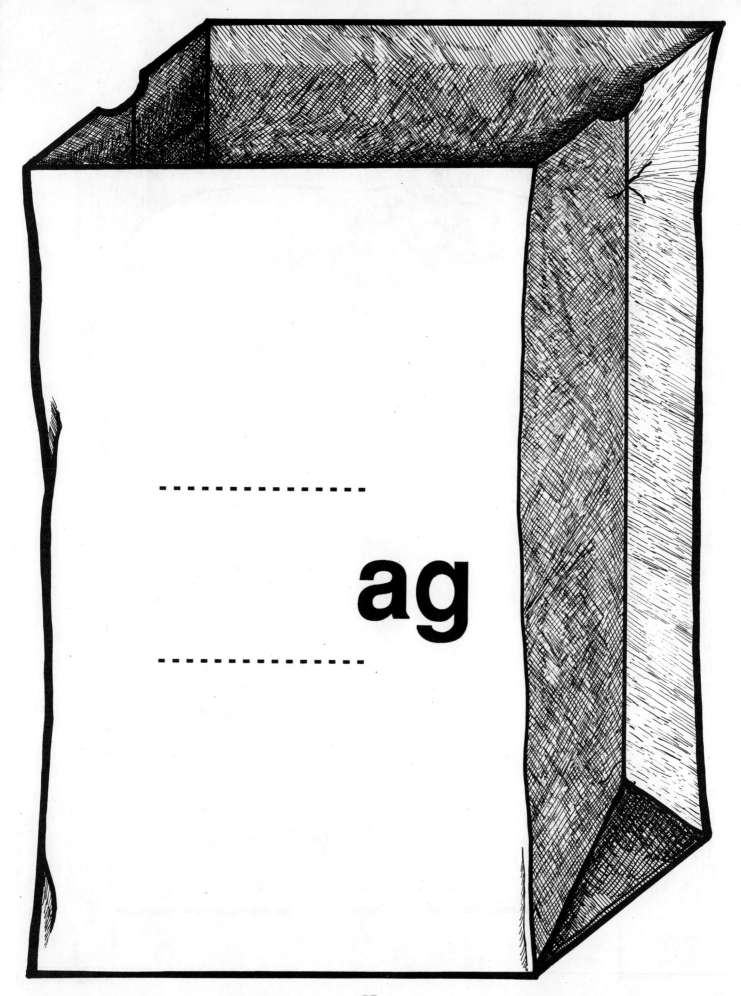

_____

ag

_____

GA1143

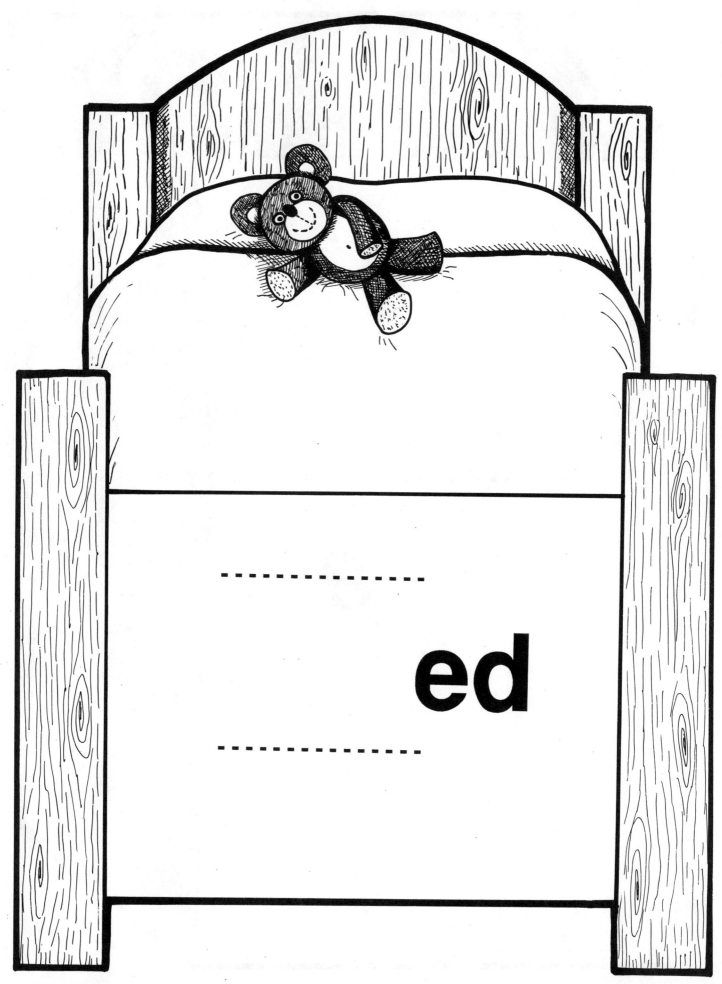

ed

56

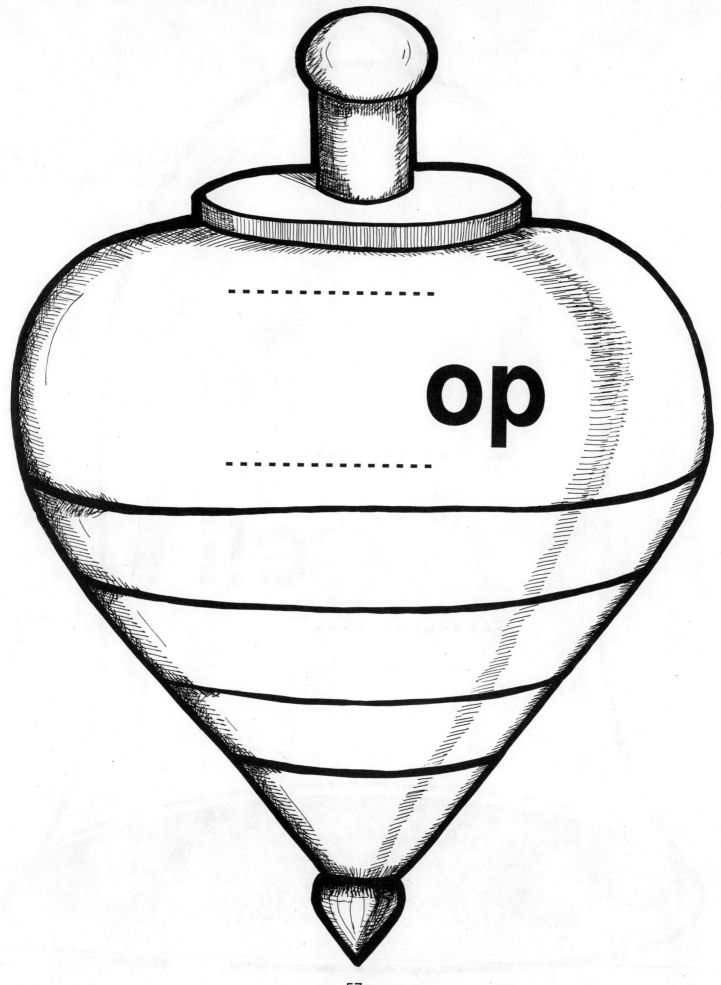

op

57

GA1143

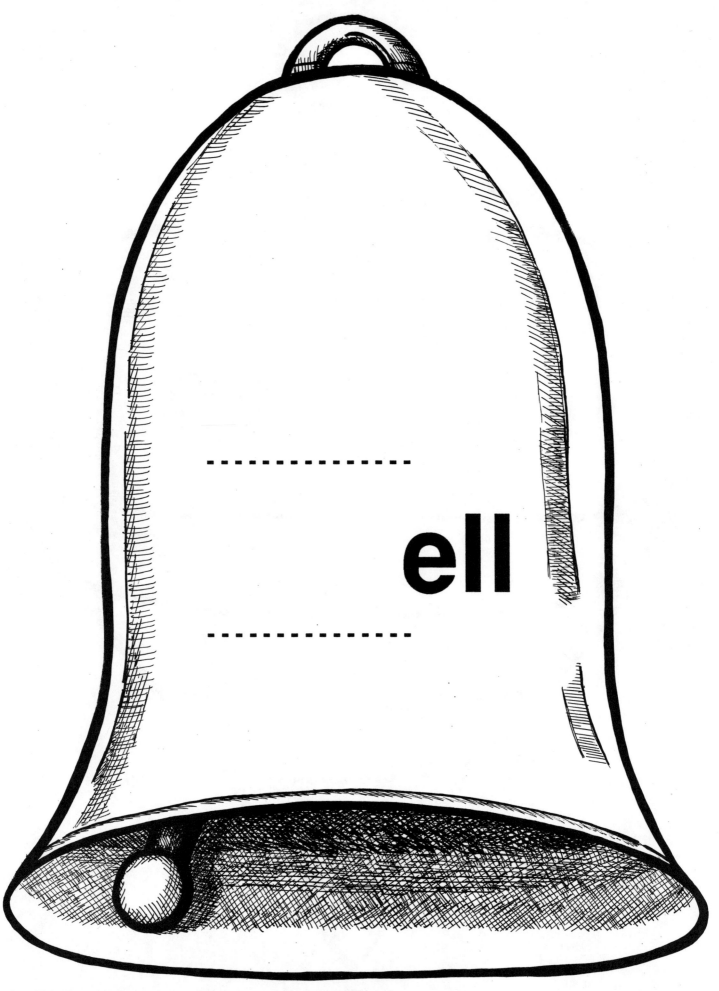

----

ell

ar

59

GA1143

ee

GA1143

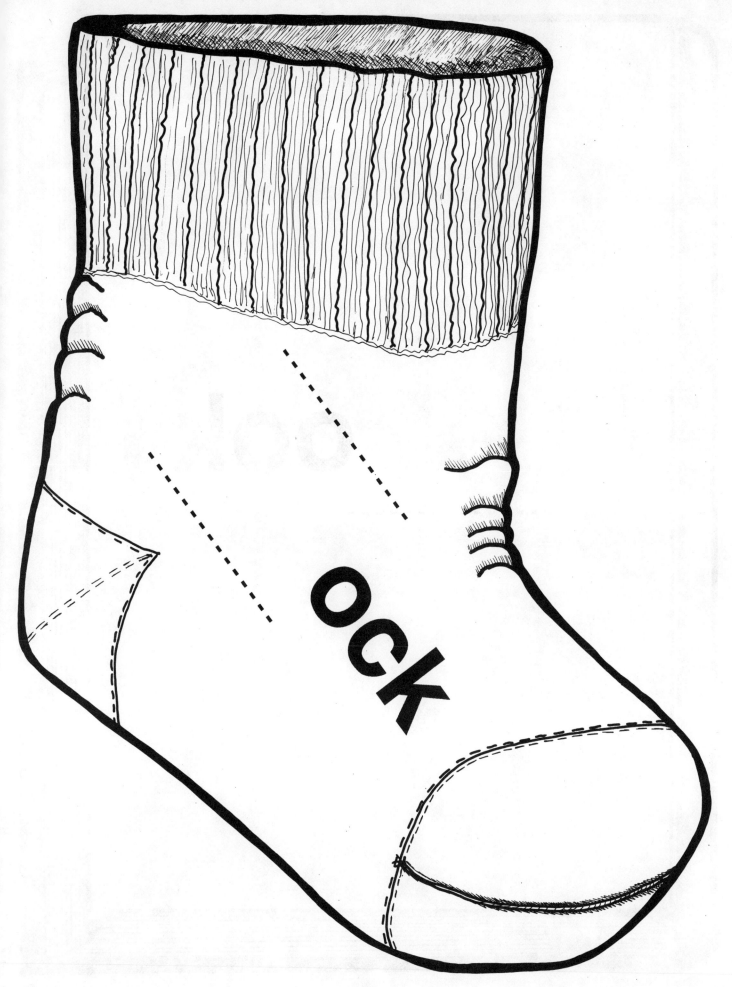

61

_____

ook

_____

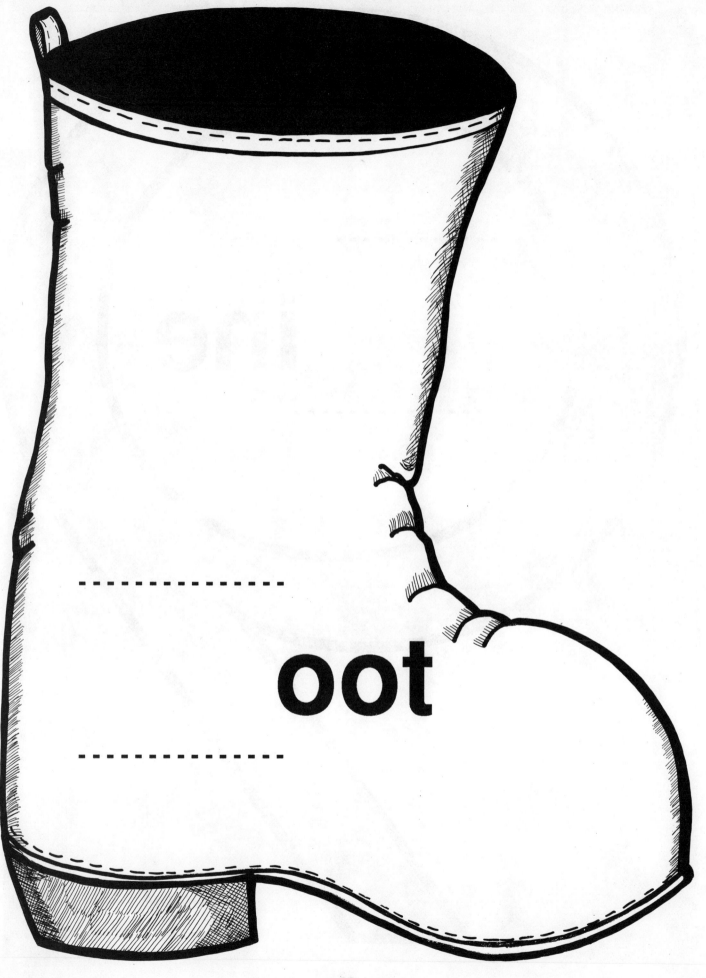

oot

GA1143

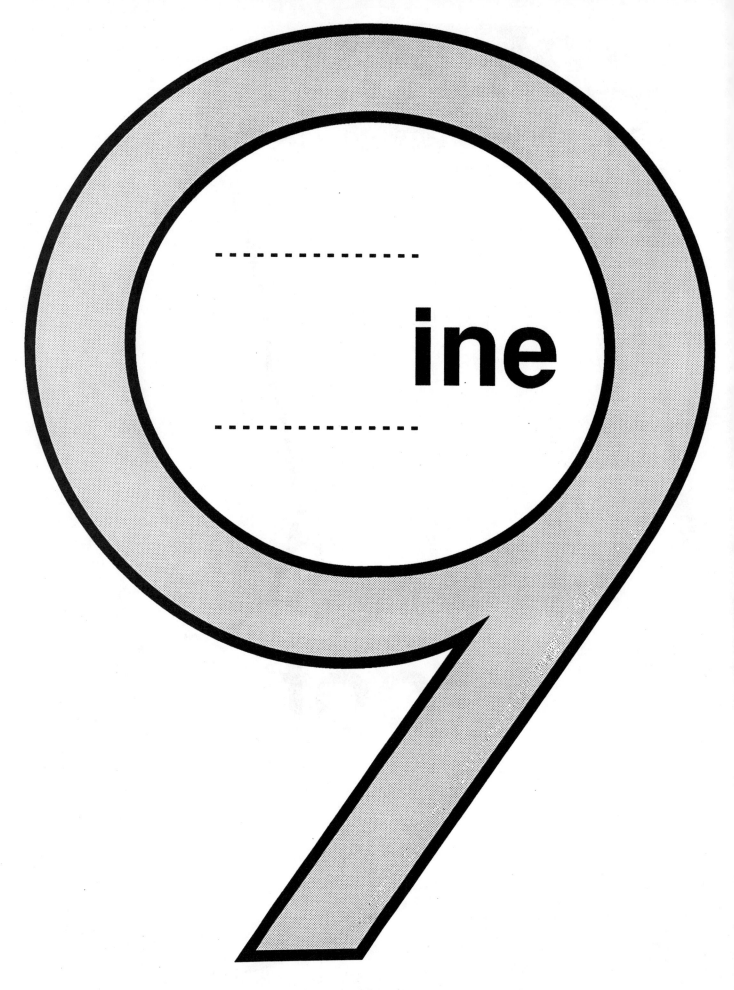

ine

64

PHONICS ENJOY CARDS

The two **BINGO style** sets of cards on pages 73-86 may be used to teach a variety of phonics (and other language) skills. **Each set** contains twenty-eight cards (seven pages with four cards each) which may be photocopied from this book and prepared for permanent use by learners. This may be done by pasting each cut card onto slightly larger heavy paper and laminating or covering with clear self-adhesive paper. The pictures on each card may be colored (if desired), or each column (or just column letters) may be highlighted with a different shade. Consider practicing with an extra photocopy.

Set A is intended to build phonics skills of beginning and final single consonant sounds and the short vowel sounds. **Set B** is intended to build the phonics skills of initial consonant blends or digraphs and the long vowel sounds. Suggested rounds for other selected language skills are also included for both sets. For example, Activities 13-16 for Set A and Activities 9-12 for Set B involve the associations of **meanings** with the pictured items, thus reinforcing the overall reading competence of the learners.

The activities are similar to **BINGO** except that every player can cover a picture **each time** an item is called (provided the appropriate **association** is made). Therefore, since the same twenty-four pictures are on each card (in mixed fashion within skill columns), the covering of all pictures **in any one column** would **not** constitute a win. Winning arrangements might be straight across, either diagonal, four corners, or **a creative combination.** An example would be letter shapes such as **N** which would cover all squares in the first and last columns and the appropriate diagonal. Others might be **X, L, U, Z, Y, T, E, F, H,** or **+.** Prior to each game, consider letting one student decide what the winning arrangement will be for that game.

Note also that this is **not** a gambling activity.

To proceed through the activity, the leader distributes one card to each player. "Tabs" are also distributed. These may be small pieces of construction paper or other covering items for the small squares on the cards. If players are unfamiliar with the bingo game style, the concept of the activity should be explained. Activity 1 for each set may be used for this purpose. (This activity simply uses the **names** of the pictures.) The leader identifies a column and then gives a language clue for a word in that column. Example: "Place a tab over a picture in column E which has the short **i** sound." (This is Activity 6-A.) Each player who can make the association of short **i** and the picture of the pig will place a tab over the pig.

The game continues until one player fills the row or shape which has been selected as a possible winning design. That player is declared the winner for that round and a new round may be played. The tabs are removed from the cards of all players before a new round is started.

On the following pages are some suggestions for rounds for both sets of cards. Additional rounds for all activities may be prepared by the group leader or the players. Feel free to expand as needed for selected groups or individuals. Above all, remember that this activity should be an ENJOYable experience!

*For written **instructional objectives** for the suggested activities, please fill in the question mark area with the name of the activity (excluding the information in parentheses): "The learner will engage in an experience which will build the language subskill of (?)." For example, for Activity 9-A, the objective will be: "The learner will engage in an experience which will build the language subskill of **short vowel sounds**."*

GA1143

Activity 1-A: Picture Concepts

Suggested wording for the leader: In column (?)* place a tab over the picture of a:

E	N	J	O	Y
HAT	CAP	BAT	CAN	FAN
BED	WELL	WEB	BELL	NET
PIG	PIN	(free)	LID	BIB
TOP	LOCK	SOCK	MOP	DOLL
SUN	BUS	GUN	DUCK	CUP

*Each time this question mark appears (in all activities for both sets), the game leader will decide which column to select (**E, N, J, O,** or **Y**) and will then choose **any one** of the five items listed beneath that column letter. Items should be selected **in mixed order.** Items which have been called may be checked with light pencil in order to avoid duplication. (These marks may be erased before the next round.) The "free" item is automatically covered on all cards for all games.

Activity 2-A: Beginning Single Consonant Sounds (Introductory Round)

In column (?) place a tab over the picture whose name begins with the sound: (Voice each sound.)

E	N	J	O	Y
\ h \ *	\ k \	\ b \	\ k \	\ f \
\ b \	\ w \	\ w \	\ b \	\ n \
\ p \	\ p \	(free)	\ l \	\ b \
\ t \	\ l \	\ s \	\ m \	\ d \
\ s \	\ b \	\ g \	\ d \	\ k \

*The answers for each item in Activities 2-16 for both sets correspond to the words listed in

Activity 1. For example, the \ h \ corresponds to the word/picture **hat.**

Activity 3-A: Beginning Single Consonant Sounds (Easier Round)

In column (?) place a tab over the picture whose name has the same beginning sound as the word:

E	N	J	O	Y
he	coat	bow	cove	fee
by	way	we	bee	no
pay	pie	(free)	lie	base
tea	low	say	me	day
see	boy	go	do	cake

This round is easier than Activity 4-A because none of the other sounds in the stimulus word are contained **in any other word** in that column. The learner needs only to make the association with the specified sound in the word pronounced with the picture.

Activity 4-A: Beginning Single Consonant Sounds (Harder Round)

In column (?) place a tab over the picture whose name has the same beginning sound as the word:

E	N	J	O	Y
head	cop	bun	cod	fib
big	win	won	bid	nap
pat	pal	(free)	luck	bet
ton	lap	sat	man	den
sat	bell	got	doll	cot

This round **forces** the positional auditory discrimination of the sound and its match with the picture word. In column **O,** for example, the

GA1143

word **cod** matches the beginning sound of the word **can**. The two other sounds in **cod** actually occur in the words **mop** and **lid**, therefore forcing the learner to consider both the specific sound utterance and its position in the words called.

Activity 5-A:
Final Single
Consonant Sounds
(Introductory Round)

In column (?) place a tab over the picture whose name ends with the sound:

E	N	J	O	Y
\ t \	\ p \	\ t \	\ n \	\ n \
\ d \	\ l \	\ b \	\ l \	\ t \
\ g \	\ n \	(free)	\ d \	\ b \
\ p \	\ k \	\ k \	\ p \	\ l \
\ n \	\ s \	\ n \	\ k \	\ p \

When voicing the above sounds, do not add a vowel sound in the utterance. Some of these sounds, such as \ p \, will be "unvoiced." Players will need to be very attentive for these sounds.

Activity 6-A:
Final Single
Consonant Sounds
(Easier Round)

In column (?) place a tab over the picture whose name has the same ending sound as the word:

E	N	J	O	Y
oat	jeep	eat	seen	mean
aid	heel	tube	fail	heat
league	mean	(free)	seed	globe
ape	ache	oak	peep	sail
own	ice	lean	seek	peep

Activity 7-A:
Final Single Consonant
Sounds (Harder Round)

In column (?) place a tab over the picture whose name has the same ending sound as the word:

E	N	J	O	Y
bit	lip	wet	mean	nun
hid	pill	sob	kill	kit
tag	ban	(free)	bad	cab
hip	pick	sack	lip	bill
tan	less	sin	lick	dip

Activity 8-A: Short Vowel Sounds

In column (?) place a tab over the picture whose name has the vowel sound:

E	N	J	O	Y
\ a \	\ a \	\ a \	\ a \	\ a \
\ e \	\ e \	\ e \	\ e \	\ e \
\ i \	\ i \	(free)	\ i \	\ i \
\ o *	\ o \	\ o \	\ o \	\ o \
\ u *	\ u \	\ u \	\ u \	\ u \

*For the purpose of simplicity, the symbols \ o \ and \ u \ will represent short **o** and short **u** respectively. The other symbols are commonly found in most dictionaries as shown.

Activity 9-A: Short Vowel Sounds

In column (?) place a tab over the picture whose name has the vowel sound:

E	N	J	O	Y
Short *a*	Short *a*	Short *a*	Short *a*	Short *a*
Short *e*	Short *e*	Short *e*	Short *e*	Short *e*
Short *i*	Short *i*	(free)	Short *i*	Short *i*
Short *o*	Short *o*	Short *o*	Short *o*	Short *o*
Short *u*	Short *u*	Short *u*	Short *u*	Short *u*

GA1143

Activity 10-A:
Medial Vowel Sounds
(Easier Round)

In column (?) place a tab over the picture whose name has the same vowel sound as the word:

E	N	J	O	Y
jam	dad	mad	fat	sack
fell	yet	fed	egg	mess
kill	him	(free)	it	is
mom	jog	cop	hot	of
cuff	hut	hum	us	hug

This round is easier than Activity 11 because none of the consonant sounds in the stimulus word are contained in any other word in that column. The learner needs only to make the association with the specified vowel sound in the word pronounced with the picture.

Activity 11-A:
Medial Vowel Sounds
(Harder Round)

In column (?) place a tab over the picture whose name has the same vowel sound as the word:

E	N	J	O	Y
pad	pack	sack	bad	nap
pet	less	bet	deck	fell
bit	wick	(free)	mill	fin
pod	pop	got	dock	not
tug	luck	buck	mud	fun

*Activity 11-A is more difficult for the learner because the consonant sounds in the stimulus word are found in other words in the column. For example, the word **pad** should be matched with **hat** because of their identical vowel sounds. The consonant sounds \ p \ and \ d \ are also found in the pictures **pig** and **bed**—thus forcing*

the learner to attend to the vowel element in the word.

Activity 12-A:
Rhyming Words

In column (?) place a tab over the picture whose name rhymes with:

E	N	J	O	Y
mat	gap	cat	ran	man
wed	tell	ebb	sell	set
jig	tin	(free)	hid	rib
cop	dock	rock	hop	loll
run	fuss	fun	tuck	pup

Activity 13-A:
Conceptual
Categorizations

In column (?) place a tab over the picture which would be appropriately placed in the category (group):

E
Things to wear, Furniture, Animals, Toys, Celestial bodies

N
Things to wear, Water source, Gadgets, Security devices, Vehicles

J
Sports equipment, Networks, Things to wear, Weapons

O
Containers, Noisemakers, Cookware, Cleanup equipment, Birds

Y
Electrical equipment, "Catching" equipment, Things to wear, Toys, Drinking containers

GA1143

Activity 14-A: Noting Characteristics or Specific Details

In column (?) place a tab over the picture which might have (a):

E

Band, Headboard, Curly tail, Spinner, Light

N

Bill, Roof, Sharp point, Keyhole, Windows

J

Tape for grip, "Threads," Heel/toe, Trigger

O

Food contents, Short handle, Knob, Strings, Feathers

Y

Electrical cord, Intersecting mesh cords, Strings to tie around neck, Hair, Curved handle

Activity 15-A: Riddles (Easier Round)

In column (?) place a tab over the picture which is the answer to the riddle:

E

I am worn on the head.
People sleep in me.
I live on a farm.
I often go for a "spin."
I am in the sky.

N

Many baseball players wear me.
I help people get water.
I fasten things together.
I help keep things from being stolen.
I take people for a ride.

J

I hit both softballs and baseballs.
A spider uses me to trap food.
I am worn on feet.
Bullets are used in me.

O

I am a food container.
I am rung in school or church.

I am placed on pots.
I help clean floors.
I quack.

Y

I help make rooms cooler.
I can help catch fish.
Babies wear me.
Children play with me.
People drink coffee in me.

Activity 16-A: Riddles (Harder Round)

In column (?) place a tab over the picture which is the answer to the riddle:

E

I am tipped at ladies.
My sizes are twin, double, queen, and king.
I provide breakfast meat.
I help entertain children.
I help plants grow.

N

I keep the sun out of eyes.
People toss pennies in me and make a wish.
I can "stick" people.
I make people feel safer.
I can help people travel from place to place.

J

I keep some people "swinging."
I am very carefully woven.
Sometimes I get lost in the washing machine.
I can be very dangerous if not used carefully.

O

I am usually thrown in the trash when I'm empty.
My sound is used to help get attention.
I help control escape of steam.
I am used with an unpopular cleaning chore.
I lived on Old MacDonald's Farm.

Y

I help control temperatures.
I help catch birds and butterflies.
I help keep clothes cleaner.
I can cry, talk, and "wet."
I am cleaned in dishwashers.

GA1143

Activity 1-B: Picture Concepts

In column (?) place a tab over the picture of:

E	N	J	O	Y
SKATE	CHAIN	SNAIL	TRAIN	SNAKE
SHEEP	THREE	TREE	WHEEL	CHEESE
FLY	KNIFE	(free)	SLIDE	BRIDE
GHOST	STOVE	SPIDER	SNOWMAN	GLOBE
MUSIC	MULE	SMOKE	CUPID	Q

Activity 2-B:
Initial Consonant Teams*
Blends and Digraphs
(Introductory Round)

In column (?) place a tab over the picture whose name begins with the sound(s):

E	N	J	O	Y
\ sk **	\ ch \	\ sn \	\ tr \	\ sn \
\ sh \	\ thr \	\ tr \	\ hw \	\ ch \
\ fl \	\ n \	(free)	\ sl \	\ br \
\ g \	\ st \	\ sp \	\ sn \	\ gl \
\ my \	\ my \	\ sm \	\ ky \	\ ky \

*The word **team** is used in Activities 2-4 to include both blends and digraphs.

The "answers" for each item choice for Activities 2-12 in Set B will correspond to the words listed in Activity 1-B. For example, the \ sk \ corresponds to the word/picture **skate.

Additional phonics information: Set B includes selected initial consonant blends and digraphs. These phonics concepts are taught differently in various classroom settings. The SOUNDS (rather than the terminology) are stressed with this activity; i.e., the words **mule, music, cupid,** and "Q" all begin with consonant blends (either \ my \ or \ ky \ ). However, labeling these as blends is not crucial to this exercise. It is also possible for students to make appropriate responses by simply auditorily discriminating only the **first** sound of some of the blends in this activity.

Activity 3-B:
Initial Consonant Teams
Blends and Digraphs
(Easier Round)

In column (?) place a tab over the picture whose name has the same initial sound(s) as the word:

E	N	J	O	Y
skin	chap	sniff	trash	snap
shove	through	trout	which	chip
flounder	now	(free)	slab	brim
give	stick	spud	snag	glue
mural	mutiny	smash	Cuba	cute

Activity 4-B:
Initial Consonant Teams
Blends and Digraphs
(Harder Round)

In column (?) place a tab over the picture whose name has the same initial sound(s) as the word:

E	N	J	O	Y
ski	chief	snowed	tried	sneeze
shy	thrive	trail	white	change
flee	knee	(free)	slain	breeze
gate	stain	spoke	snail	glide
mute	mucus	smile	cute	cured

SPECIAL NOTE: For the following four activities, the vowel sounds of ONLY THE FIRST SYLLABLE in the words **music, spider, snowman,** and **cupid** are to be matched. This should be explained prior to each activity.

GA1143

Activity 5-B: Long Vowel Sounds (Introductory Round)

In column (?) place a tab over the picture whose name has the vowel sound:

E	N	J	O	Y
\ a \	\ a \	\ a \	\ a \	\ a \
\ e \	\ e \	\ e \	\ e \	\ e \
\ i \	\ i \	(free)	\ i \	\ i \
\ o \	\ o \	\ i \	\ o \	\ o \
\ yu *	\ yu \	\ o \	\ yu \	\ yu \

*Note: The symbols \ yu \ represent the conventionally named "long u" sound because this "sound" consists of both the initial consonant sound of \ y \ and the vowel sound \ u \.

Activity 6-B: Long Vowel Sounds

In column (?) place a tab over the picture whose name has the vowel sound:

E	N	J	O	Y
Long a	Long a	Long a	Long a	Long a
Long e	Long e	Long e	Long e	Long e
Long i	Long i	(free)	Long i	Long i
Long o	Long o	Long i	Long o	Long o
Long u	Long u	Long o	Long u	Long u

Activity 7-B: Long Vowel Sounds (Easier Round)

In column (?) place a tab over the picture whose name has the same vowel sound as the word:

E	N	J	O	Y
way	day	hay	bay	may
we	he	fee	be	me
high	die	(free)	by	why
no	doe	guy	go	toe
cute	Cuba	foe	you	few

Activity 8-B: Long Vowel Sounds (Harder Round)

In column (?) place a tab over the picture whose name has the same vowel sound as the word:

E	N	J	O	Y
shape	stale	trail	stayed	glaze
ski	kneel	speed	sleet	Greek
sky	thrive	(free)	trial	skies
scope	known	tried	slowed	broke
pew	future	snowed	feud	view

Activity 9-B: Conceptual Categorizations

Place a tab over the picture which would be appropriately placed in the category (group):

E
Footwear,
Animals, Insects,
Apparitions or "Spirits,"
Entertainment

N
Linked objects,
Numbers, Pocket tools,
Appliances, Animals

J
Small animals,
Plants, Insects,
Air pollutants

O
Vehicles, Moving Parts,
Playground equipment,
Cold-weather characters,
Valentine characters

Y
Reptiles, Food,
Persons, Earth models,
Alphabet

GA1143

Activity 10-B: Noting Characteristics or Specific Details

In column (?) place a tab over the picture which might have (a) (an):

E

Wheels, Wool, Wings, Haunting effects, Notes

N

Links, Two curves and three points, Blades, Heating elements, Ears

J

Spiral shell, Leaves, Spinnerets, Carbon particles

O

Engine, Spokes, Ladder, Carrot nose, Bow and arrow

Y

Fangs, "Holes," Veil, Sphere, An "O" shape with a tail

Activity 11-B: Riddles (Easier Round)

In column (?) place a tab over the picture which is the answer to the riddle:

E

I love to roll over smooth surfaces.
Little Bo Peep lost me.
People try to swat me.
I frighten many people.
People use me while singing.

N

I am jewelry worn around the neck.
It takes this many strikes to be out in baseball.
I'm used to cut things.
I help cook meals.
I live on a farm.

J

I'm slow and sometimes slimy.
I lose my leaves in winter.
My bite can be poisonous.
I'm always around fire.

O

I move on two rails.

I'm round and make things move more easily.
Coming down me is more fun than going up.
I usually don't "live" but just a short time.
I help people fall in love.

Y

I crawl on my belly.
I taste good with crackers.
You can't have a wedding without me.
I'm a round map of the world.
I come before "r."

Activity 12-B: Riddles (Harder round)

In column (?) place a tab over the picture which is the answer to the riddle:

E

If you don't use me carefully, you'll fall down!
People count me to help go to sleep at night.
I buzz around picnic food.
I appear at Halloween!
I'm played on the radio.

N

I'm used to tow cars.
How many blind mice were there?
Be very careful closing me!
I have two to four "eyes."
People say I'm very stubborn.

J

I'm part of what little boys are made of.
I'm not a dog, but I have bark!
My weaving catches flies.
Like Santa Claus, I go up the chimney.

O

Sometimes I hold up traffic.
There are two of me on a bicycle.
There's a sudden stop at the end of me.
The sun just kills me!
Valentine's Day is fun for me.

Y

My fangs are dangerous.
People put me in mousetraps.
I like to wear a long dress and veil.
I spin around but never get dizzy.
I'm almost always followed by "u."

GA1143

Card 1, Set A

Card 2, Set A

Card 3, Set A

Card 4, Set A

GA1143

See pages 65-72 for preparation instructions and activities for this sheet.

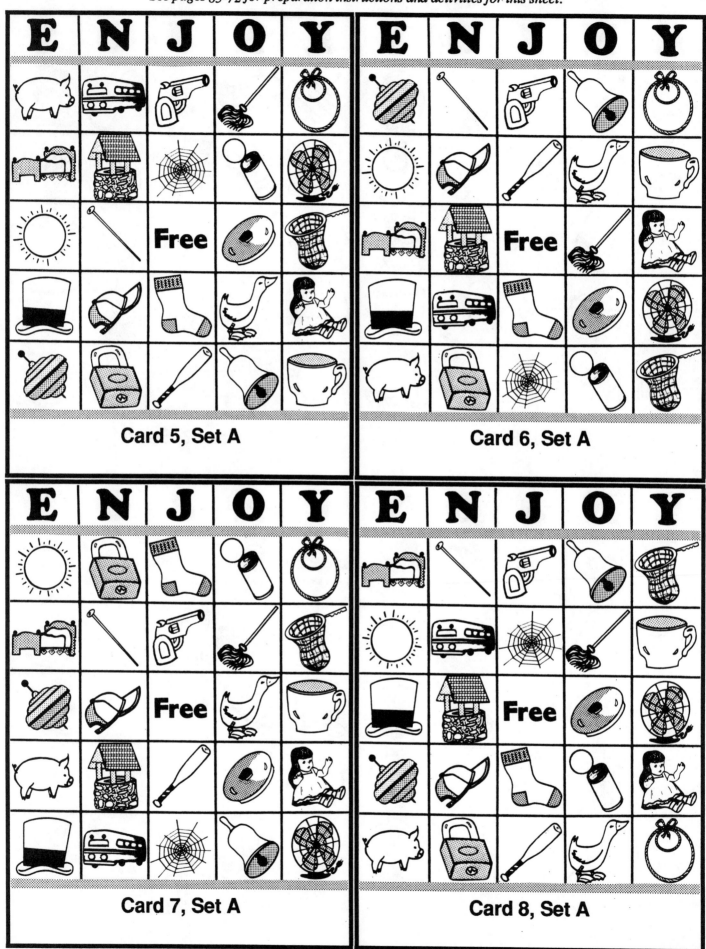

Card 5, Set A

Card 6, Set A

Card 7, Set A

Card 8, Set A

GA1143

Card 9, Set A

Card 10, Set A

Card 11, Set A

Card 12, Set A

GA1143

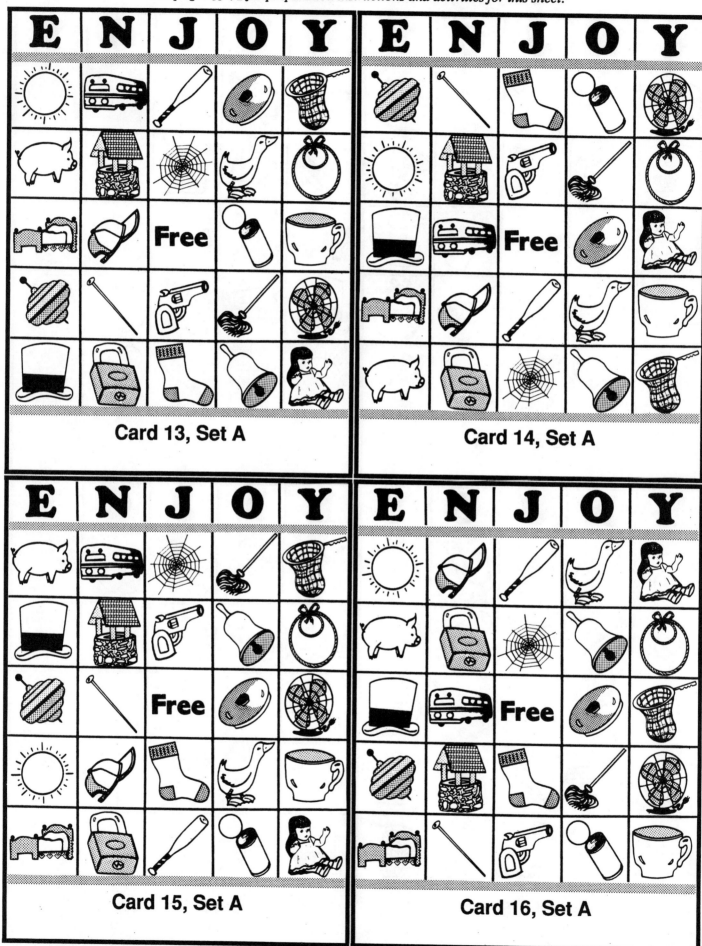

Card 13, Set A

Card 14, Set A

Card 15, Set A

Card 16, Set A

76

GA1143

See pages 65-72 for preparation instructions and activities for this sheet.

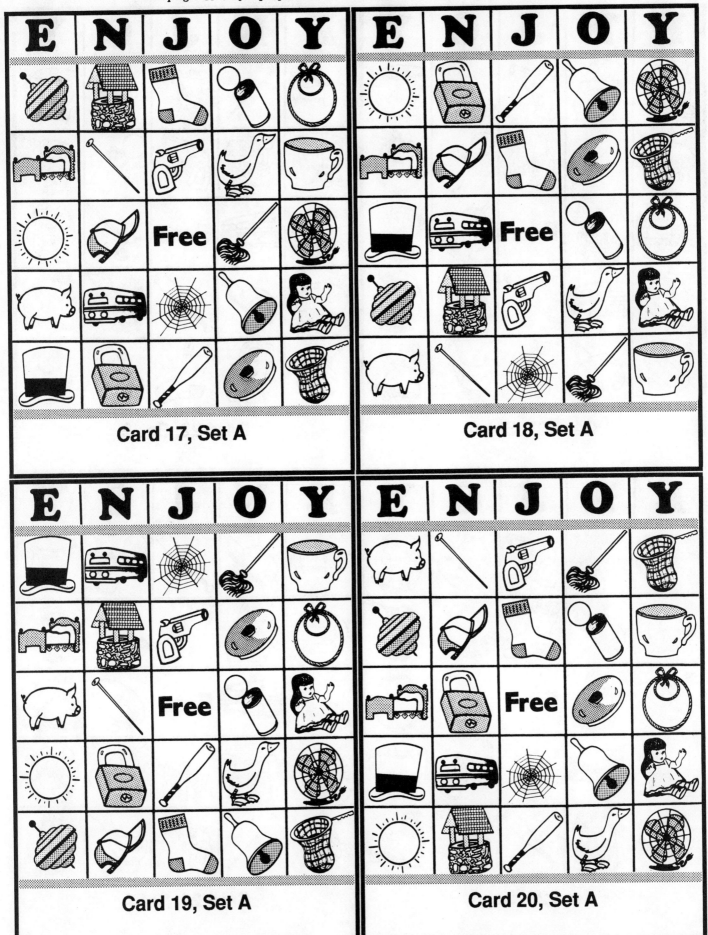

Card 17, Set A

Card 18, Set A

Card 19, Set A

Card 20, Set A

77

GA1143

Card 21, Set A

Card 22, Set A

Card 23, Set A

Card 24, Set A

78

Card 25, Set A

Card 26, Set A

Card 27, Set A

Card 28, Set A

GA1143

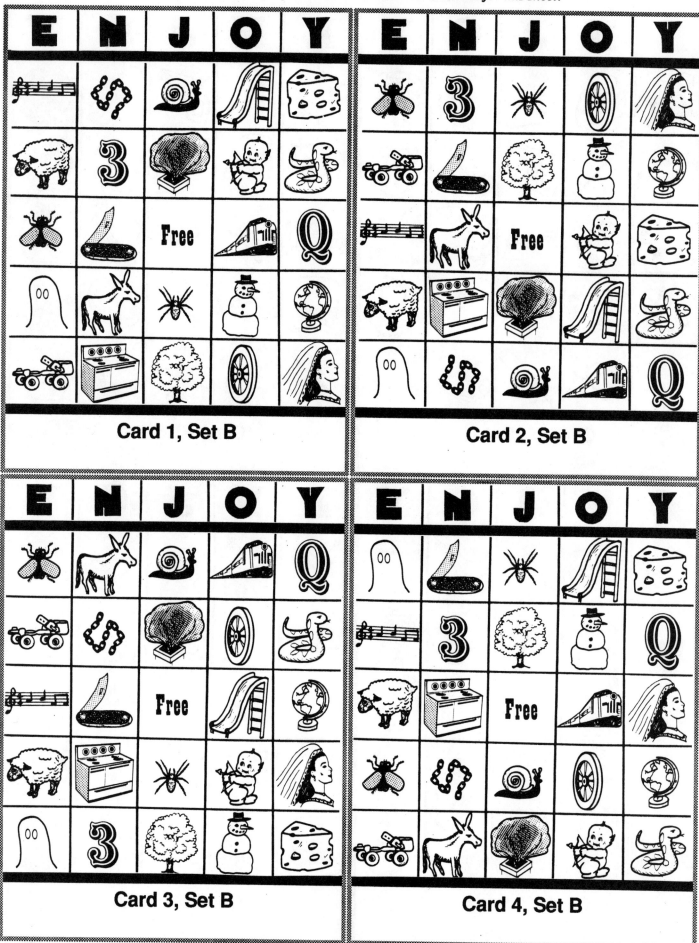

Card 1, Set B

Card 2, Set B

Card 3, Set B

Card 4, Set B

GA1143

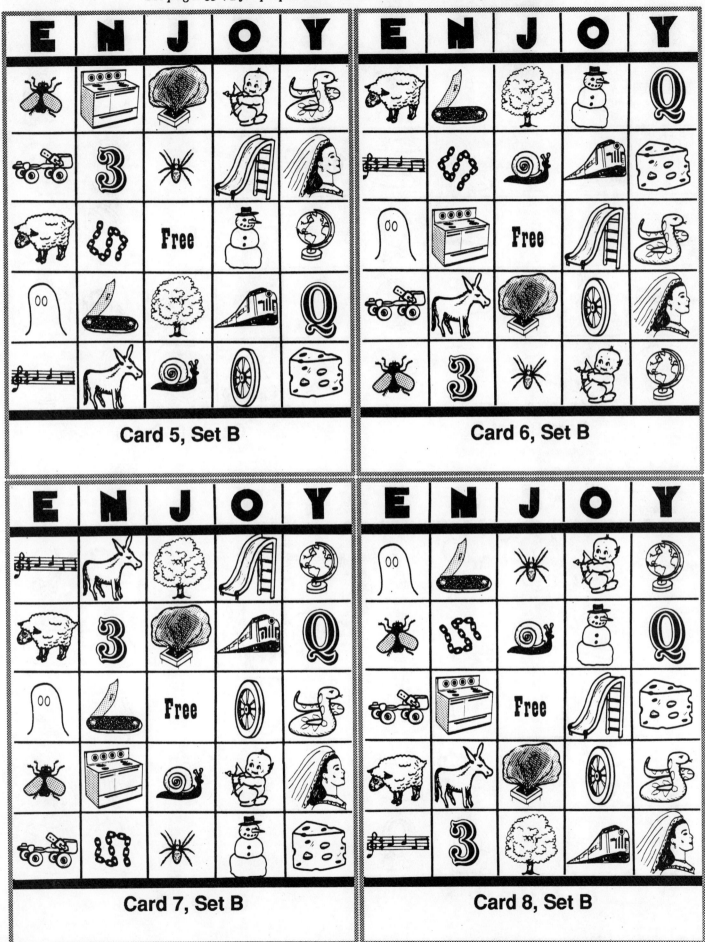

Card 5, Set B

Card 6, Set B

Card 7, Set B

Card 8, Set B

GA1143

Card 9, Set B

Card 10, Set B

Card 11, Set B

Card 12, Set B

GA1143

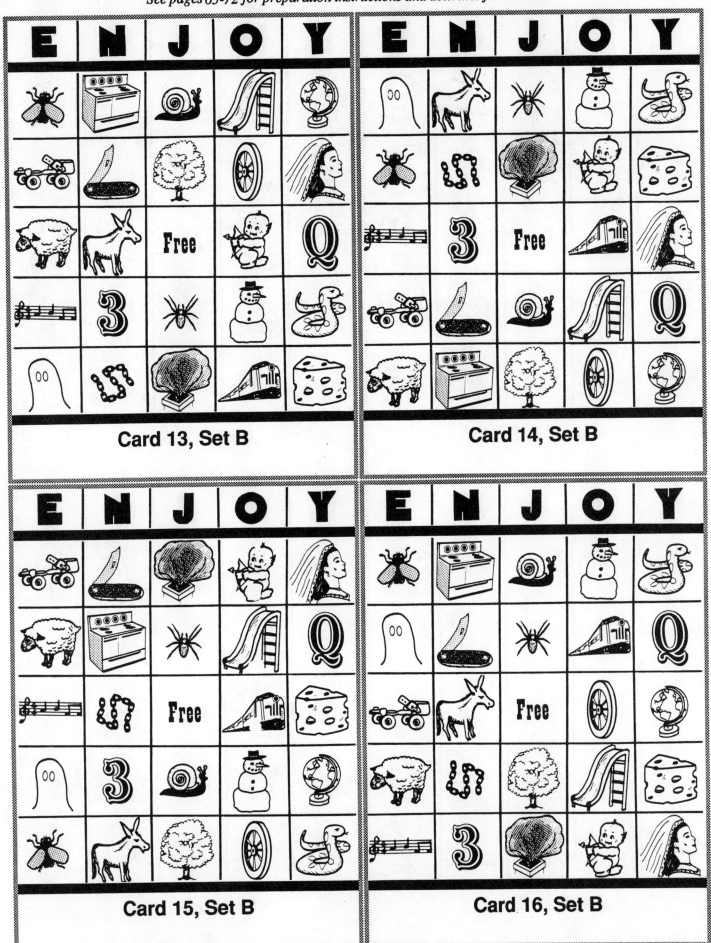

Card 13, Set B

Card 14, Set B

Card 15, Set B

Card 16, Set B

GA1143

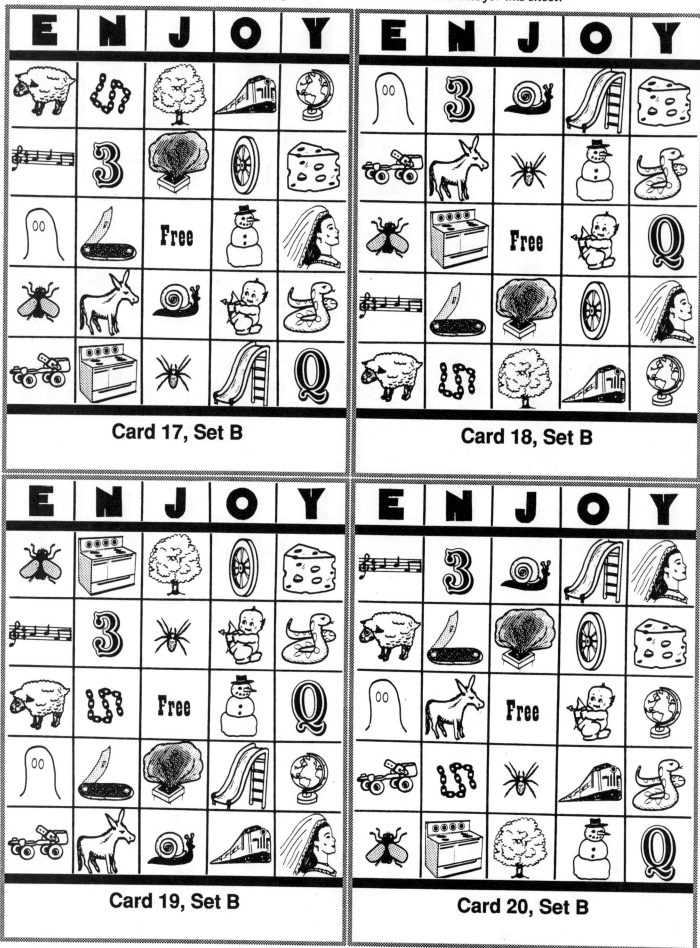

Card 17, Set B

Card 18, Set B

Card 19, Set B

Card 20, Set B

84

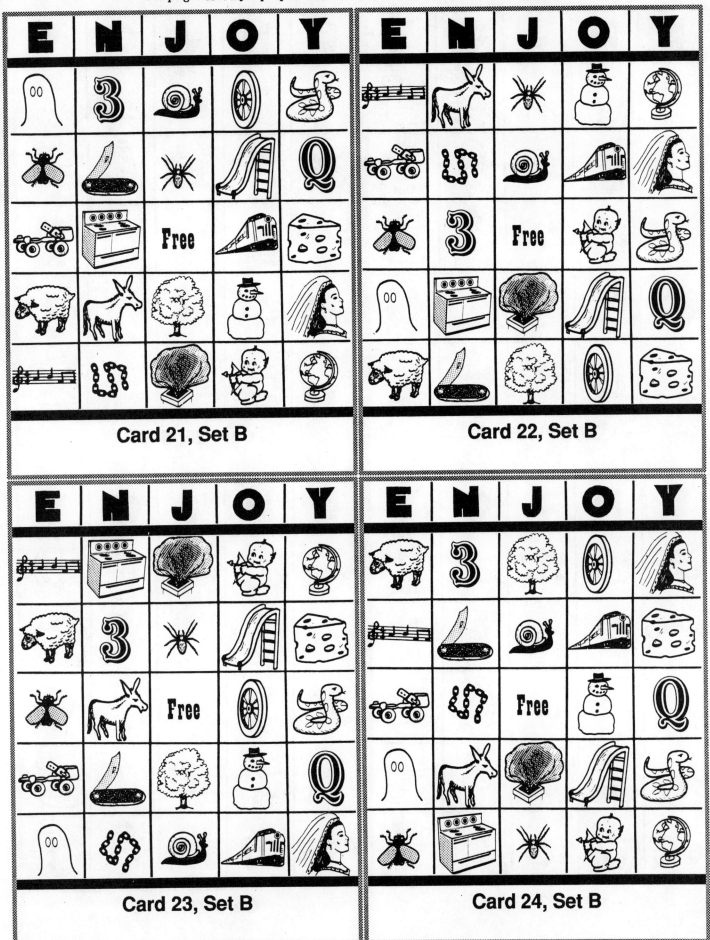

Card 21, Set B

Card 22, Set B

Card 23, Set B

Card 24, Set B

GA1143

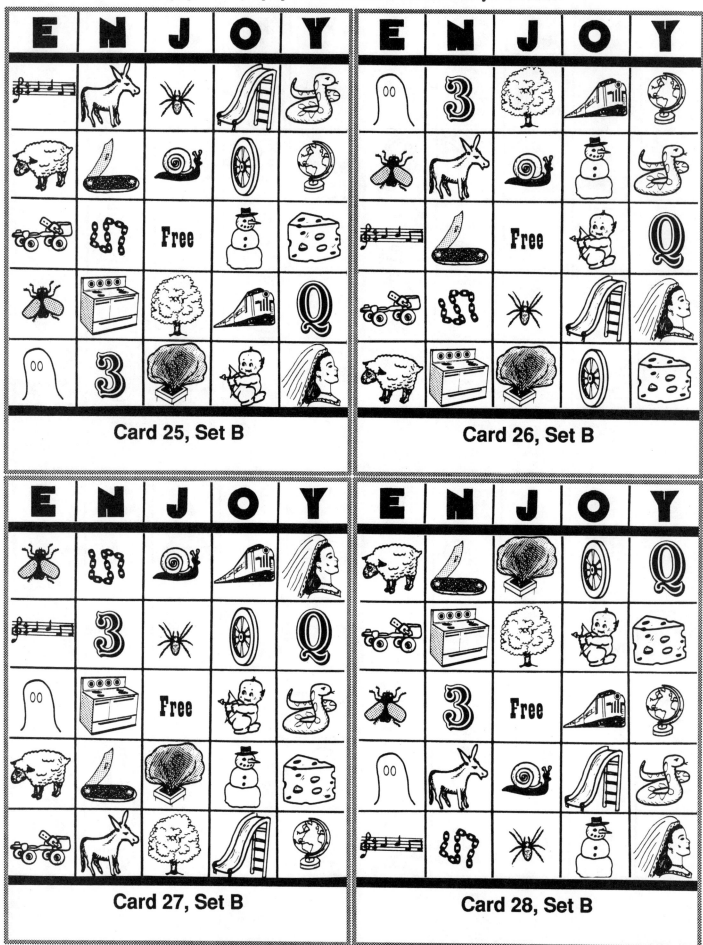

Card 25, Set B

Card 26, Set B

Card 27, Set B

Card 28, Set B

GA1143

SECTION 5

PHONICS MINI-CARDS

Various small card activities may be prepared for building the basic phonics principles with young learners. Two different types of small cards are presented on pages 93-142 for a variety of purposes. One type is called *Phonics Question Mini-Cards*. The other type is called *Phonics Letter Mini-Cards*. Duplicate sets of these cards may be made through careful photocopying; however, caution is given to align the fronts and backs of these pages carefully. Below is information regarding these two types of cards.

Phonics Question Mini-Cards

Preparation: The *Phonics Question Mini-Cards* may be prepared by cutting out pages 93-122. Carefully remove the pages from this text by cutting on the dotted lines. (Do not tear the sheets from the text. Tearing may cause the corresponding front pages to fall loose.) If desired, laminate these pages or cover them with clear self-adhesive paper. Then carefully cut out each separate card pictured on the page.

Storing: The cards from each separate page may be housed different ways. One method is to place each set in a small envelope or a library card pocket. Each envelope should be labeled for ease in distribution of the cards. Another method is to prepare a small box according to the guide shown on page 92. Card dividers (also shown on page 92) may be used to separate each of the sets.

Description: Each page of the *Phonics Question Mini-Cards* contains twenty cards prepared for building one specific phonics skill. Ten of these cards have a clear background. An additional ten cards are identical except for having a shaded background. These "twin" sets allow competition between teams or individuals by presenting equal information to both.

Activities: A variety of activities may be used with these cards. One suggestion is to give the unshaded cards from one set to a player (or team) and the shaded cards from the same set to another player. The phonics skill is explained to both sides and any desired discussion may occur. When the leader says "go," each player places his cards one at a time into two separate labeled containers (boxes, baskets, or designated tabletop areas). One container is designated for one skill (such as "b" for pictures which start with the letter **b**) and the other area for the contrasting skill (such as "d" for pictures which start with the letter **d**). The mini-signs on page 144 may be used for this purpose.

GA1143

As soon as one player finishes placing all of his cards in the corresponding containers, the other player stops, setting aside his remaining unplaced cards. One point is given (for both players) for each card which was dropped into the correct container. The points are recorded and the cards are returned **in mixed order** (keeping the shaded and unshaded cards separate) to the envelope or box file. New rounds may be played and the points accumulate. The winner is the one with the highest accumulated points.

The scoring may be modified in any way desired. For example, a point may also be **subtracted** for any **incorrectly** placed cards, or one point may be added for each unused card remaining in the opponent's hand.

Other activities may also occur with these cards. Players may work independently, constantly checking the answers on the backs of the cards. No competition occurs with this style of activity. Learning is self-paced and the skills are self-correcting.

Create as many new activities as desired. Keep in mind that students may prepare their own sets of *Phonics Question Mini-Cards*. Using photocopies of page 123 and the answer sides of any of the prepared rounds (or the blank answer page on 124), students may create many additional sets by locating/drawing pictures or by writing words which fit a specific phonics subskill. Much learning will occur as they prepare new rounds.

Skills: Each page of cards may be used to build a separate phonics subskill. The following are the specific objectives for these pages.

Page 93: Learner will determine whether the word represented by a picture has the single initial consonant b or d.

Page 95: Learner will determine whether the word represented by a picture has the final single consonant t or g.

Page 97: Learner will determine whether the word represented by a picture has the long i or the short i vowel sound.

Page 99: Learner will determine whether the word represented by a picture has the initial consonant blend represented by letters br or cr.

Page 101: Learner will determine whether the word represented by a picture has final consonant sound(s) represented by the letters ck or st.

Page 103: Learner will determine whether the word represented by a picture has the ee or the ea spelling for the sound of the vowel.

Page 105: Learner will determine whether the word represented by a picture has the ou or the ow spelling for the sound of the vowel.

Page 107: Learner will determine whether the word represented by a picture has one or two syllables.

Page 109: Learner will determine whether a printed word has one or two syllables.

Page 111: Learner will determine whether a printed word has a long or a short vowel sound.

Page 113: Learner will determine whether a printed word has a hard c or a soft c sound.

Page 115: Learner will determine whether a printed word has a hard g or a soft g sound.

Page 117: Learner will determine whether a printed word rhymes with the word good or food.

Page 119: Learner will determine whether a printed word rhymes with the word wed or weed.

Page 121: Learner will determine whether a printed word rhymes with the word ear or her.

Page 123: This page is blank. The instructor or players may prepare cards for any desired phonics objective.

Phonics Letter Mini-Cards

The mini-cards on pages 125-142 contain letters for building specific phonics skills. They may be prepared in a manner similar to the *Phonics Question Mini-Cards*. Guides for a container to house these cards and guides for optional dividers are shown on page 92. Optional divider labels are shown on page 144.

A multitude of different phonics activities may be used with these cards. Below are some suggestions. Note that the word **selected** is used in many activity descriptions. Please select only those cards containing phonic elements with which the players are familiar. Also, the cards used for some activities may be placed on the tabletop **either with the letters showing or face down with the letters hidden.** This will be the choice of the game leader and will affect the difficulty of the game. When the cards are placed facedown, the game may be played "concentration" style, and players may keep the single or matching cards as they make correct responses or matches. When desired, scoring may be figured by the number of cards each player has accumulated by the end of the round.

Instructional Objectives: Specific objectives may be written for each of the Activities 2-10 below by using the following wording: "The learner will build the phonics subskill of making appropriate associations of letters and sounds involving (??)." (Fill in the question marks with the activity name.)

Activity 1: Pre-phonics—Matching Uppercase and Lowercase Letters

Place the uppercase and the lowercase letter cards on a tabletop. Have players take turns matching these letters by picking up two cards at a time and determining if they match.

Activity 2: Initial Single Consonant Sounds

Place selected lowercase consonant cards on a tabletop. Have players (one at a time) pick up a card and say a word which **begins** with that letter/sound.

Activity 3: Initial Single Consonant Sounds

Select one lowercase consonant card. Show it to all players. At an indicated starting time have players say as many words as possible which begin with that consonant. One point is given to the **first** player to say each **new** word within a specified time limit. Continue with additional consonant cards.

Activity 4: Final Single Consonant Sounds

Place selected lowercase consonant cards on a tabletop. Have players pick up a card (one at a time) and say a word which **ends** with that consonant. *(Be sure to omit the **h, w, and y** cards from activities involving final consonant sounds because these letters do not represent consonant sounds in the final positions of words/syllables.)*

Activity 5: Final Single Consonant Sounds

Select one lowercase consonant card. Show it to all players. At an indicated starting time have players say as many words as possible which end with that consonant. One point is given to the **first** player to say each **new** word within a specified time limit. Continue with additional consonant cards.

GA1143

Activity 6: Single Consonant Sounds

Place selected lowercase consonant cards on a tabletop. Have players (one at a time) pick up a card and say a word which contains that letter/sound **anywhere** in the word.

*(Note that for many of the following activities the word **team** is frequently used. Young learners are better able to grasp this term than the words **digraph** or **blend**. Any appropriate desired terminology may be used.)*

Activity 7: Vowel Teams (Digraphs)

*(The vowel letter team cards included are **-ai-, -au-, -aw-, -ay-, -ea-, -ee-, -ei-, -ey-, -oa-, -oi-, -oo-, -ou-, -ow-, -oy-, -ar-, -er-, -ir-, -or-,** and **-ur-**. Although the "r-influenced" vowel teams contain the consonant letter **r**, this is a logical place to include them. If desired, these five cards could be moved to the phonogram section.)*
Place selected vowel team cards on a tabletop. Have players (one at a time) pick up a card and say a word which contains that vowel team (digraph) **in any position** within a word.

Activity 8: Vowel Teams (Digraphs)

Select one vowel team card. Show it to all players. At an indicated starting time have players say as many words as possible which contain that vowel team. One point is given to the **first** player to say each **new** word within a specified time limit. Continue with additional vowel team cards.

Activity 9: Initial Consonant Teams (Blends and Digraphs)

*(The consonant team cards included are **bl-, br-, ch-, cl-, cr-, dr-, fl-, fr-, gh-, gl-, gr-, kn-, ph-, pl-, pr-, sc-, scr-, sh-, sl-, sm-, sn-, sp-, spl-, spr-, st-, str-, sw-, th-, thr-, tr-, tw-, wh-,** and **wr-**.)*
Place selected consonant team cards on a tabletop. Have players (one at a time) pick up a card and say a word which contains that **initial** consonant team (blend or digraph)

Activity 10: Initial Consonant Teams (Blends and Digraphs)

Select one consonant team card. Show it to all players. At an indicated starting time have players say as many words as possible which contain that consonant team. One point is given to the **first** player to say each **new** word within a specified time limit. Continue with additional consonant team cards.

Activity 11: Phonogram Fun

*(A phonogram is a cluster of letters generally forming numerous words when initial consonant sounds are added. The phonogram cards included are **-ab** on page 133 and all cards on the remaining pages. The hyphen reminds learners that letters should be added to the beginning of the phonogram.)*

GA1143

Select one phonogram card. Show it to all players. At an indicated starting time have players say as many words as possible which contain that phonogram. One point is given to the **first** player to say each **new** word within a specified time limit. Continue with additional phonogram cards.

Activity 12: Phonograms and Single Consonants

Place selected single consonant cards on a tabletop. To the right of these cards, place selected phonogram cards. Have players pick up a single consonant card and a phonogram card which will form a word. The player says the word aloud. The players continue until no more matches can be made. (The used cards may either be kept by the players for scoring purposes or may be returned for greater word possibilities.)

Activity 13: Phonograms and Initial Consonant Teams

Place selected consonant team cards on a tabletop. To the right of these cards, place selected phonogram cards. Have players pick up a consonant team card and a phonogram card which will form a word. The player says the word aloud. The players continue until no more matches can be made. (The used cards may either be kept by the players for scoring purposes or may be returned for greater word possibilities.)

Activity 14: Phonics/Spelling Games

Distribute selected single letter cards (or team cards) among all players. Pronounce a word. Have players having the needed letters to spell that word stand and hold them in a position to show the "printed" word.

Many additional activities may be used with these cards. Explore the use of the blank cards (page 143 and any earlier page back) to allow players to prepare additional mini-cards for phonics. You are limited only to your own imagination and to the abilities of the players. **HAVE FUN!**

91 GA1143

Guides for Boxes and Dividers

Box guide for *Phonics Question Mini-Cards*

1. Cut box guides from six-ply heavy paper.
2. Crease with a razor blade at dotted lines.
3. Tape into box shape.
4. Cover with decorative paper.

Box guide for *Phonics Letter Mini-Cards*

Divider guides

GA1143

Begins with
<u>b</u> or <u>d</u>?

Begins with
<u>b</u> or <u>d</u>?

Begins with
<u>b</u> or <u>d</u>?

Begins with
<u>b</u> or <u>d</u>?

Begins with
<u>b</u> or <u>d</u>?

Begins with
<u>b</u> or <u>d</u>?

Begins with
<u>b</u> or <u>d</u>?

Begins with
<u>b</u> or <u>d</u>?

Begins with
<u>b</u> or <u>d</u>?

Begins with
<u>b</u> or <u>d</u>?

Begins with
<u>b</u> or <u>d</u>?

Begins with
<u>b</u> or <u>d</u>?

Begins with
<u>b</u> or <u>d</u>?

Begins with
<u>b</u> or <u>d</u>?

Begins with
<u>b</u> or <u>d</u>?

Begins with
<u>b</u> or <u>d</u>?

Begins with
<u>b</u> or <u>d</u>?

Begins with
<u>b</u> or <u>d</u>?

Begins with
<u>b</u> or <u>d</u>?

Cut on dotted line. See pages 87-92 for preparation instructions and activities for this sheet.

GA1143

Answer:

d

(duck)

Set 1

Answer:

b

(bed)

Set 1

Answer:

d

(duck)

Set 1

Answer:

b

(bed)

Set 1

Answer:

d

(dinosaur)

Set 1

Answer:

b

(boat)

Set 1

Answer:

d

(dinosaur)

Set 1

Answer:

b

(boat)

Set 1

Answer:

d

(dice)

Set 1

Answer:

b

(beans)

Set 1

Answer:

d

(dice)

Set 1

Answer:

b

(beans)

Set 1

Answer:

d

(deer)

Set 1

Answer:

b

(basketball)

Set 1

Answer:

d

(deer)

Set 1

Answer:

b

(basketball)

Set 1

Answer:

d

(dime)

Set 1

Answer:

b

(boy)

Set 1

Answer:

d

(dime)

Set 1

Answer:

b

(boy)

Set 1

GA1143

Ends with
<u>t</u> or <u>g</u>?

Ends with
<u>t</u> or <u>g</u>?

Ends with
<u>t</u> or <u>g</u>?

Ends with
<u>t</u> or <u>g</u>?

Ends with
<u>t</u> or <u>g</u>?

Ends with
<u>t</u> or <u>g</u>?

Ends with
<u>t</u> or <u>g</u>?

Ends with
<u>t</u> or <u>g</u>?

Ends with
<u>t</u> or <u>g</u>?

Ends with
<u>t</u> or <u>g</u>?

Ends with
<u>t</u> or <u>g</u>?

Ends with
<u>t</u> or <u>g</u>?

Ends with
<u>t</u> or <u>g</u>?

Ends with
<u>t</u> or <u>g</u>?

Ends with
<u>t</u> or <u>g</u>?

Ends with
<u>t</u> or <u>g</u>?

Ends with
<u>t</u> or <u>g</u>?

Ends with
<u>t</u> or <u>g</u>?

Ends with
<u>t</u> or <u>g</u>?

GA1143

Answer:
g
(bag)
Set 2

Answer:
t
(rabbit)
Set 2

Answer:
g
(bag)
Set 2

Answer:
t
(rabbit)
Set 2

Answer:
g
(leg)
Set 2

Answer:
t
(hat)
Set 2

Answer:
g
(leg)
Set 2

Answer:
t
(hat)
Set 2

Answer:
g
(flag)
Set 2

Answer:
t
(coat)
Set 2

Answer:
g
(flag)
Set 2

Answer:
t
(coat)
Set 2

Answer:
g
(frog)
Set 2

Answer:
t
(paint)
Set 2

Answer:
g
(frog)
Set 2

Answer:
t
(paint)
Set 2

Answer:
g
(tag)
Set 2

Answer:
t
(eight)
Set 2

Answer:
g
(tag)
Set 2

Answer:
t
(eight)
Set 2

GA1143

Has long i
or short i?

Has long i
or short i?

Has long i
or short i?

Has long i
or short i?

Has long i
or short i?

Has long i
or short i?

Has long i
or short i?

Has long i
or short i?

Has long i
or short i?

Has long i
or short i?

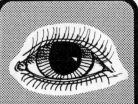

Has long i
or short i?

Has long i
or short i?

Has long i
or short i?

Has long i
or short i?

Has long i
or short i?

Has long i
or short i?

Has long i
or short i?

Has long i
or short i?

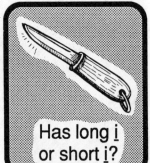

Has long i
or short i?

Has long i
or short i?

Answer:
short i
(pig)
Set 3

Answer:
long i
(pie)
Set 3

Answer:
short i
(pig)
Set 3

Answer:
long i
(pie)
Set 3

Answer:
short i
(fish)
Set 3

Answer:
long i
(tie)
Set 3

Answer:
short i
(fish)
Set 3

Answer:
long i
(tie)
Set 3

Answer:
short i
(ring)
Set 3

Answer:
long i
(eye)
Set 3

Answer:
short i
(ring)
Set 3

Answer:
long i
(eye)
Set 3

Answer:
short i
(bill)
Set 3

Answer:
long i
(pipe)
Set 3

Answer:
short i
(bill)
Set 3

Answer:
long i
(pipe)
Set 3

Answer:
short i
(lips)
Set 3

Answer:
long i
(knife)
Set 3

Answer:
short i
(lips)
Set 3

Answer:
long i
(knife)
Set 3

GA1143

Begins with <u>br</u> or <u>cr</u>?

Begins with <u>br</u> or <u>cr</u>?

Begins with <u>br</u> or <u>cr</u>?

Begins with <u>br</u> or <u>cr</u>?

Begins with <u>br</u> or <u>cr</u>?

Begins with <u>br</u> or <u>cr</u>?

Begins with <u>br</u> or <u>cr</u>?

Begins with <u>br</u> or <u>cr</u>?

Begins with <u>br</u> or <u>cr</u>?

Begins with <u>br</u> or <u>cr</u>?

Begins with <u>br</u> or <u>cr</u>?

Begins with <u>br</u> or <u>cr</u>?

Begins with <u>br</u> or <u>cr</u>?

Begins with <u>br</u> or <u>cr</u>?

Begins with <u>br</u> or <u>cr</u>?

Begins with <u>br</u> or <u>cr</u>?

Begins with <u>br</u> or <u>cr</u>?

Begins with <u>br</u> or <u>cr</u>?

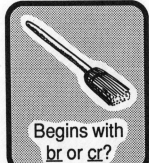

Begins with <u>br</u> or <u>cr</u>?

Begins with <u>br</u> or <u>cr</u>?

Cut on dotted line. See pages 87-92 for preparation instructions and activities for this sheet.

GA1143

Answer: **cr** (crab) Set 4

Answer: **br** (bridge) Set 4

Answer: **cr** (crab) Set 4

Answer: **br** (bridge) Set 4

Answer: **cr** (cross) Set 4

Answer: **br** (brick) Set 4

Answer: **cr** (cross) Set 4

Answer: **br** (brick) Set 4

Answer: **cr** (cry) Set 4

Answer: **br** (bracelet) Set 4

Answer: **cr** (cry) Set 4

Answer: **br** (bracelet) Set 4

Answer: **cr** (crayons) Set 4

Answer: **br** (bread) Set 4

Answer: **cr** (crayons) Set 4

Answer: **br** (bread) Set 4

Answer: **cr** (crutches) Set 4

Answer: **br** (broom) Set 4

Answer: **cr** (crutches) Set 4

Answer: **br** (broom) Set 4

100

GA1143

Ends with
<u>ck</u> or <u>st</u>?

Ends with
<u>ck</u> or <u>st</u>?

Ends with
<u>ck</u> or <u>st</u>?

Ends with
<u>ck</u> or <u>st</u>?

Ends with
<u>ck</u> or <u>st</u>?

Ends with
<u>ck</u> or <u>st</u>?

Ends with
<u>ck</u> or <u>st</u>?

Ends with
<u>ck</u> or <u>st</u>?

Ends with
<u>ck</u> or <u>st</u>?

Ends with
<u>ck</u> or <u>st</u>?

Ends with
<u>ck</u> or <u>st</u>?

Ends with
<u>ck</u> or <u>st</u>?

Ends with
<u>ck</u> or <u>st</u>?

Ends with
<u>ck</u> or <u>st</u>?

Ends with
<u>ck</u> or <u>st</u>?

Ends with
<u>ck</u> or <u>st</u>?

Ends with
<u>ck</u> or <u>st</u>?

Ends with
<u>ck</u> or <u>st</u>?

Ends with
<u>ck</u> or <u>st</u>?

Ends with
<u>ck</u> or <u>st</u>?

GA1143

Answer:
st
(toast)
Set 5

Answer:
ck
(check)
Set 5

Answer:
st
(toast)
Set 5

Answer:
ck
(check)
Set 5

Answer:
st
(fist)
Set 5

Answer:
ck
(truck)
Set 5

Answer:
st
(fist)
Set 5

Answer:
ck
(truck)
Set 5

Answer:
st
(ghost)
Set 5

Answer:
ck
(clock)
Set 5

Answer:
st
(ghost)
Set 5

Answer:
ck
(clock)
Set 5

Answer:
st
(vest)
Set 5

Answer:
ck
(neck)
Set 5

Answer:
st
(vest)
Set 5

Answer:
ck
(neck)
Set 5

Answer:
st
(nest)
Set 5

Answer:
ck
(block)
Set 5

Answer:
st
(nest)
Set 5

Answer:
ck
(block)
Set 5

GA1143

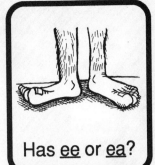
Has <u>ee</u> or <u>ea</u>?

Has <u>ee</u> or <u>ea</u>?

Has <u>ee</u> or <u>ea</u>?

Has <u>ee</u> or <u>ea</u>?

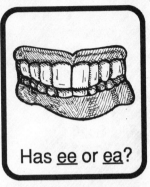
Has <u>ee</u> or <u>ea</u>?

Has <u>ee</u> or <u>ea</u>?

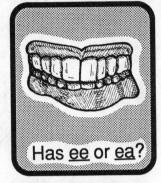
Has <u>ee</u> or <u>ea</u>?

Has <u>ee</u> or <u>ea</u>?

15
Has <u>ee</u> or <u>ea</u>?

Has <u>ee</u> or <u>ea</u>?

15
Has <u>ee</u> or <u>ea</u>?

Has <u>ee</u> or <u>ea</u>?

Has <u>ee</u> or <u>ea</u>?

Has <u>ee</u> or <u>ea</u>?

Has <u>ee</u> or <u>ea</u>?

Has <u>ee</u> or <u>ea</u>?

Has <u>ee</u> or <u>ea</u>?

Has <u>ee</u> or <u>ea</u>?

Has <u>ee</u> or <u>ea</u>?

Has <u>ee</u> or <u>ea</u>?

Cut on dotted line. See pages 87-92 for preparation instructions and activities for this sheet.

GA1143

Answer:
ea
(seal)
Set 6

Answer:
ee
(feet)
Set 6

Answer:
ea
(seal)
Set 6

Answer:
ee
(feet)
Set 6

Answer:
ea
(peach)
Set 6

Answer:
ee
(teeth)
Set 6

Answer:
ea
(peach)
Set 6

wer:
ee
(teeth)
Set 6

Answer:
ea
(leaf)
Set 6

Answer:
ee
(fifteen)
Set 6

Answer:
ea
(leaf)
Set 6

Answer:
ee
(fifteen)
Set 6

Answer:
ea
(peas)
Set 6

Answer:
ee
(bee)
Set 6

Answer:
ea
(peas)
Set 6

Answer:
ee
(bee)
Set 6

Answer:
ea
(ice cream)
Set 6

Answer:
ee
(heel)
Set 6

Answer:
ea
(ice cream)
Set 6

Answer:
ee
(heel)
Set 6

GA1143

Has <u>ou</u> or <u>ow</u>?

Has <u>ou</u> or <u>ow</u>?

Has <u>ou</u> or <u>ow</u>?

Has <u>ou</u> or <u>ow</u>?

Has <u>ou</u> or <u>ow</u>?

Has <u>ou</u> or <u>ow</u>?

Has <u>ou</u> or <u>ow</u>?

Has <u>ou</u> or <u>ow</u>?

Has <u>ou</u> or <u>ow</u>?

Has <u>ou</u> or <u>ow</u>?

Has <u>ou</u> or <u>ow</u>?

Has <u>ou</u> or <u>ow</u>?

Has <u>ou</u> or <u>ow</u>?

Has <u>ou</u> or <u>ow</u>?

Has <u>ou</u> or <u>ow</u>?

Has <u>ou</u> or <u>ow</u>?

Has <u>ou</u> or <u>ow</u>?

Has <u>ou</u> or <u>ow</u>?

Has <u>ou</u> or <u>ow</u>?

Has <u>ou</u> or <u>ow</u>?

GA1143

Answer:
ow
(crown)
Set 7

Answer:
ou
(mouse)
Set 7

Answer:
ow
(crown)
Set 7

Answer:
ou
(mouse)
Set 7

Answer:
ow
(clown)
Set 7

Answer:
ou
(cloud)
Set 7

Answer:
ow
(clown)
Set 7

Answer:
ou
(cloud)
Set 7

Answer:
ow
(cow)
Set 7

Answer:
ou
(blouse)
Set 7

Answer:
ow
(cow)
Set 7

Answer:
ou
(blouse)
Set 7

Answer:
ow
(frown)
Set 7

Answer:
ou
(house)
Set 7

Answer:
ow
(frown)
Set 7

Answer:
ou
(house)
Set 7

Answer:
ow
(brow)
Set 7

Answer:
ou
(mouth)
Set 7

Answer:
ow
(brow)
Set 7

Answer:
ou
(mouth)
Set 7

GA1143

Has <u>one</u> or <u>two</u> syllables?

Has <u>one</u> or <u>two</u> syllables?

Has <u>one</u> or <u>two</u> syllables?

Has <u>one</u> or <u>two</u> syllables?

Has <u>one</u> or <u>two</u> syllables?

Has <u>one</u> or <u>two</u> syllables?

Has <u>one</u> or <u>two</u> syllables?

Has <u>one</u> or <u>two</u> syllables?

Has <u>one</u> or <u>two</u> syllables?

Has <u>one</u> or <u>two</u> syllables?

Has <u>one</u> or <u>two</u> syllables?

Has <u>one</u> or <u>two</u> syllables?

Has <u>one</u> or <u>two</u> syllables?

Has <u>one</u> or <u>two</u> syllables?

Has <u>one</u> or <u>two</u> syllables?

Has <u>one</u> or <u>two</u> syllables?

Has <u>one</u> or <u>two</u> syllables?

Has <u>one</u> or <u>two</u> syllables?

Has <u>one</u> or <u>two</u> syllables?

Has <u>one</u> or <u>two</u> syllables?

GA1143

Answer:
two
(monkey)
Set 8

Answer:
one
(skunk)
Set 8

Answer:
two
(monkey)
Set 8

Answer:
one
(skunk)
Set 8

Answer:
two
(turtle)
Set 8

Answer:
one
(snail)
Set 8

Answer:
two
(turtle)
Set 8

Answer:
one
(snail)
Set 8

Answer:
two
(sandwich)
Set 8

Answer:
one
(nurse)
Set 8

Answer:
two
(sandwich)
Set 8

Answer:
one
(nurse)
Set 8

Answer:
two
(mushroom)
Set 8

Answer:
one
(drum)
Set 8

Answer:
two
(mushroom)
Set 8

Answer:
one
(drum)
Set 8

Answer:
two
(apple)
Set 8

Answer:
one
(snake)
Set 8

Answer:
two
(apple)
Set 8

Answer:
one
(snake)
Set 8

GA1143

white

Has <u>one</u> or <u>two</u> syllables?

any

Has <u>one</u> or <u>two</u> syllables?

white

Has <u>one</u> or <u>two</u> syllables?

any

Has <u>one</u> or <u>two</u> syllables?

think

Has <u>one</u> or <u>two</u> syllables?

open

Has <u>one</u> or <u>two</u> syllables?

think

Has <u>one</u> or <u>two</u> syllables?

open

Has <u>one</u> or <u>two</u> syllables?

brown

Has <u>one</u> or <u>two</u> syllables?

into

Has <u>one</u> or <u>two</u> syllables?

brown

Has <u>one</u> or <u>two</u> syllables?

into

Has <u>one</u> or <u>two</u> syllables?

please

Has <u>one</u> or <u>two</u> syllables?

never

Has <u>one</u> or <u>two</u> syllables?

please

Has <u>one</u> or <u>two</u> syllables?

never

Has <u>one</u> or <u>two</u> syllables?

don't

Has <u>one</u> or <u>two</u> syllables?

yellow

Has <u>one</u> or <u>two</u> syllables?

don't

Has <u>one</u> or <u>two</u> syllables?

yellow

Has <u>one</u> or <u>two</u> syllables?

GA1143

Answer:
two
Set 9

Answer:
one
Set 9

Answer:
two
Set 9

Answer:
one
Set 9

Answer:
two
Set 9

Answer:
one
Set 9

Answer:
two
Set 9

Answer:
one
Set 9

Answer:
two
Set 9

Answer:
one
Set 9

Answer:
two
Set 9

Answer:
one
Set 9

Answer:
two
Set 9

Answer:
one
Set 9

Answer:
two
Set 9

Answer:
one
Set 9

Answer:
two
Set 9

Answer:
one
Set 9

Answer:
two
Set 9

Answer:
one
Set 9

GA1143

eight

Has <u>long</u> or <u>short</u> vowel sound?

black

Has <u>long</u> or <u>short</u> vowel sound?

eight

Has <u>long</u> or <u>short</u> vowel sound?

black

Has <u>long</u> or <u>short</u> vowel sound?

three

Has <u>long</u> or <u>short</u> vowel sound?

yes

Has <u>long</u> or <u>short</u> vowel sound?

three

Has <u>long</u> or <u>short</u> vowel sound?

yes

Has <u>long</u> or <u>short</u> vowel sound?

fly

Has <u>long</u> or <u>short</u> vowel sound?

drink

Has <u>long</u> or <u>short</u> vowel sound?

fly

Has <u>long</u> or <u>short</u> vowel sound?

drink

Has <u>long</u> or <u>short</u> vowel sound?

know

Has <u>long</u> or <u>short</u> vowel sound?

hot

Has <u>long</u> or <u>short</u> vowel sound?

know

Has <u>long</u> or <u>short</u> vowel sound?

hot

Has <u>long</u> or <u>short</u> vowel sound?

you

Has <u>long</u> or <u>short</u> vowel sound?

does

Has <u>long</u> or <u>short</u> vowel sound?

you

Has <u>long</u> or <u>short</u> vowel sound?

does

Has <u>long</u> or <u>short</u> vowel sound?

Answer:
**short
vowel
sound**

Set 10

Answer:
**long
vowel
sound**

Set 10

Answer:
**short
vowel
sound**

Set 10

Answer:
**long
vowel
sound**

Set 10

Answer:
**short
vowel
sound**

Set 10

Answer:
**long
vowel
sound**

Set 10

Answer:
**short
vowel
sound**

Set 10

Answer:
**long
vowel
sound**

Set 10

Answer:
**short
vowel
sound**

Set 10

Answer:
**long
vowel
sound**

Set 10

Answer:
**short
vowel
sound**

Set 10

Answer:
**long
vowel
sound**

Set 10

Answer:
**short
vowel
sound**

Set 10

Answer:
**long
vowel
sound**

Set 10

Answer:
**short
vowel
sound**

Set 10

Answer:
**long
vowel
sound**

Set 10

Answer:
**short
vowel
sound**

Set 10

Answer:
**long
vowel
sound**

Set 10

Answer:
**short
vowel
sound**

Set 10

Answer:
**long
vowel
sound**

Set 10

GA1143

city Has <u>hard c</u> or <u>soft c</u> sound?	**cut** Has <u>hard c</u> or <u>soft c</u> sound?	**city** Has <u>hard c</u> or <u>soft c</u> sound?	**cut** Has <u>hard c</u> or <u>soft c</u> sound?
once Has <u>hard c</u> or <u>soft c</u> sound?	**can** Has <u>hard c</u> or <u>soft c</u> sound?	**once** Has <u>hard c</u> or <u>soft c</u> sound?	**can** Has <u>hard c</u> or <u>soft c</u> sound?
cent Has <u>hard c</u> or <u>soft c</u> sound?	**came** Has <u>hard c</u> or <u>soft c</u> sound?	**cent** Has <u>hard c</u> or <u>soft c</u> sound?	**came** Has <u>hard c</u> or <u>soft c</u> sound?
cell Has <u>hard c</u> or <u>soft c</u> sound?	**carry** Has <u>hard c</u> or <u>soft c</u> sound?	**cell** Has <u>hard c</u> or <u>soft c</u> sound?	**carry** Has <u>hard c</u> or <u>soft c</u> sound?
cigar Has <u>hard c</u> or <u>soft c</u> sound?	**could** Has <u>hard c</u> or <u>soft c</u> sound?	**cigar** Has <u>hard c</u> or <u>soft c</u> sound?	**could** Has <u>hard c</u> or <u>soft c</u> sound?

GA1143

Answer:
**hard c
sound**

Set 11

Answer:
**soft c
sound**

Set 11

Answer:
**hard c
sound**

Set 11

Answer:
**soft c
sound**

Set 11

Answer:
**hard c
sound**

Set 11

Answer:
**soft c
sound**

Set 11

Answer:
**hard c
sound**

Set 11

Answer:
**soft c
sound**

Set 11

Answer:
**hard c
sound**

Set 11

Answer:
**soft c
sound**

Set 11

Answer:
**hard c
sound**

Set 11

Answer:
**soft c
sound**

Set 11

Answer:
**hard c
sound**

Set 11

Answer:
**soft c
sound**

Set 11

Answer:
**hard c
sound**

Set 11

Answer:
**soft c
sound**

Set 11

Answer:
**hard c
sound**

Set 11

Answer:
**soft c
sound**

Set 11

Answer:
**hard c
sound**

Set 11

Answer:
**soft c
sound**

Set 11

GA1143

big Has <u>hard g</u> or <u>soft g</u> sound?	**germ** Has <u>hard g</u> or <u>soft g</u> sound?	**big** Has <u>hard g</u> or <u>soft g</u> sound?	**germ** Has <u>hard g</u> or <u>soft g</u> sound?
gave Has <u>hard g</u> or <u>soft g</u> sound?	**edge** Has <u>hard g</u> or <u>soft g</u> sound?	**gave** Has <u>hard g</u> or <u>soft g</u> sound?	**edge** Has <u>hard g</u> or <u>soft g</u> sound?
good Has <u>hard g</u> or <u>soft g</u> sound?	**giant** Has <u>hard g</u> or <u>soft g</u> sound?	**good** Has <u>hard g</u> or <u>soft g</u> sound?	**giant** Has <u>hard g</u> or <u>soft g</u> sound?
fog Has <u>hard g</u> or <u>soft g</u> sound?	**giraffe** Has <u>hard g</u> or <u>soft g</u> sound?	**fog** Has <u>hard g</u> or <u>soft g</u> sound?	**giraffe** Has <u>hard g</u> or <u>soft g</u> sound?
goes Has <u>hard g</u> or <u>soft g</u> sound?	**gentle** Has <u>hard g</u> or <u>soft g</u> sound?	**goes** Has <u>hard g</u> or <u>soft g</u> sound?	**gentle** Has <u>hard g</u> or <u>soft g</u> sound?

Answer:
**soft g
sound**

Set 12

Answer:
**hard g
sound**

Set 12

Answer:
**soft g
sound**

Set 12

Answer:
**hard g
sound**

Set 12

Answer:
**soft g
sound**

Set 12

Answer:
**hard g
sound**

Set 12

Answer:
**soft g
sound**

Set 12

Answer:
**hard g
sound**

Set 12

Answer:
**soft g
sound**

Set 12

Answer:
**hard g
sound**

Set 12

Answer:
**soft g
sound**

Set 12

Answer:
**hard g
sound**

Set 12

Answer:
**soft g
sound**

Set 12

Answer:
**hard g
sound**

Set 12

Answer:
**soft g
sound**

Set 12

Answer:
**hard g
sound**

Set 12

Answer:
**soft g
sound**

Set 12

Answer:
**hard g
sound**

Set 12

Answer:
**soft g
sound**

Set 12

Answer:
**hard g
sound**

Set 12

GA1143

wood Rhymes with <u>good</u> or <u>food</u>?	**mood** Rhymes with <u>good</u> or <u>food</u>?	**wood** Rhymes with <u>good</u> or <u>food</u>?	**mood** Rhymes with <u>good</u> or <u>food</u>?
could Rhymes with <u>good</u> or <u>food</u>?	**rude** Rhymes with <u>good</u> or <u>food</u>?	**could** Rhymes with <u>good</u> or <u>food</u>?	**rude** Rhymes with <u>good</u> or <u>food</u>?
stood Rhymes with <u>good</u> or <u>food</u>?	**you'd** Rhymes with <u>good</u> or <u>food</u>?	**stood** Rhymes with <u>good</u> or <u>food</u>?	**you'd** Rhymes with <u>good</u> or <u>food</u>?
should Rhymes with <u>good</u> or <u>food</u>?	**brood** Rhymes with <u>good</u> or <u>food</u>?	**should** Rhymes with <u>good</u> or <u>food</u>?	**brood** Rhymes with <u>good</u> or <u>food</u>?
hood Rhymes with <u>good</u> or <u>food</u>?	**who'd** Rhymes with <u>good</u> or <u>food</u>?	**hood** Rhymes with <u>good</u> or <u>food</u>?	**who'd** Rhymes with <u>good</u> or <u>food</u>?

GA1143

Answer:
food
Set 13

Answer:
good
Set 13

Answer:
food
Set 13

Answer:
good
Set 13

Answer:
food
Set 13

Answer:
good
Set 13

Answer:
food
Set 13

Answer:
good
Set 13

Answer:
food
Set 13

Answer:
good
Set 13

Answer:
food
Set 13

Answer:
good
Set 13

Answer:
food
Set 13

Answer:
good
Set 13

Answer:
food
Set 13

Answer:
good
Set 13

Answer:
food
Set 13

Answer:
good
Set 13

Answer:
food
Set 13

Answer:
good
Set 13

GA1143

need

Rhymes with
<u>wed</u> or <u>weed</u>?

head

Rhymes with
<u>wed</u> or <u>weed</u>?

need

Rhymes with
<u>wed</u> or <u>weed</u>?

head

Rhymes with
<u>wed</u> or <u>weed</u>?

bead

Rhymes with
<u>wed</u> or <u>weed</u>?

bled

Rhymes with
<u>wed</u> or <u>weed</u>?

bead

Rhymes with
<u>wed</u> or <u>weed</u>?

bled

Rhymes with
<u>wed</u> or <u>weed</u>?

seed

Rhymes with
<u>wed</u> or <u>weed</u>?

dead

Rhymes with
<u>wed</u> or <u>weed</u>?

seed

Rhymes with
<u>wed</u> or <u>weed</u>?

dead

Rhymes with
<u>wed</u> or <u>weed</u>?

plead

Rhymes with
<u>wed</u> or <u>weed</u>?

said

Rhymes with
<u>wed</u> or <u>weed</u>?

plead

Rhymes with
<u>wed</u> or <u>weed</u>?

said

Rhymes with
<u>wed</u> or <u>weed</u>?

feed

Rhymes with
<u>wed</u> or <u>weed</u>?

bread

Rhymes with
<u>wed</u> or <u>weed</u>?

feed

Rhymes with
<u>wed</u> or <u>weed</u>?

bread

Rhymes with
<u>wed</u> or <u>weed</u>?

Cut on dotted line. See pages 87-92 for preparation instructions and activities for this sheet.

GA1143

Answer:
wed
Set 14

Answer:
weed
Set 14

Answer:
wed
Set 14

Answer:
weed
Set 14

Answer:
wed
Set 14

Answer:
weed
Set 14

Answer:
wed
Set 14

Answer:
weed
Set 14

Answer:
wed
Set 14

Answer:
weed
Set 14

Answer:
wed
Set 14

Answer:
weed
Set 14

Answer:
wed
Set 14

Answer:
weed
Set 14

Answer:
wed
Set 14

Answer:
weed
Set 14

Answer:
wed
Set 14

Answer:
weed
Set 14

Answer:
wed
Set 14

Answer:
weed
Set 14

GA1143

fear

Rhymes with
<u>ear</u> or <u>her</u>?

sir

Rhymes with
<u>ear</u> or <u>her</u>?

fear

Rhymes with
<u>ear</u> or <u>her</u>?

sir

Rhymes with
<u>ear</u> or <u>her</u>?

deer

Rhymes with
<u>ear</u> or <u>her</u>?

were

Rhymes with
<u>ear</u> or <u>her</u>?

deer

Rhymes with
<u>ear</u> or <u>her</u>?

were

Rhymes with
<u>ear</u> or <u>her</u>?

here

Rhymes with
<u>ear</u> or <u>her</u>?

fir

Rhymes with
<u>ear</u> or <u>her</u>?

here

Rhymes with
<u>ear</u> or <u>her</u>?

fir

Rhymes with
<u>ear</u> or <u>her</u>?

year

Rhymes with
<u>ear</u> or <u>her</u>?

purr

Rhymes with
<u>ear</u> or <u>her</u>?

year

Rhymes with
<u>ear</u> or <u>her</u>?

purr

Rhymes with
<u>ear</u> or <u>her</u>?

steer

Rhymes with
<u>ear</u> or <u>her</u>?

slur

Rhymes with
<u>ear</u> or <u>her</u>?

steer

Rhymes with
<u>ear</u> or <u>her</u>?

slur

Rhymes with
<u>ear</u> or <u>her</u>?

GA1143

Answer:
her
Set 15

Answer:
ear
Set 15

Answer:
her
Set 15

Answer:
ear
Set 15

Answer:
her
Set 15

Answer:
ear
Set 15

Answer:
her
Set 15

Answer:
ear
Set 15

Answer:
her
Set 15

Answer:
ear
Set 15

Answer:
her
Set 15

Answer:
ear
Set 15

Answer:
her
Set 15

Answer:
ear
Set 15

Answer:
her
Set 15

Answer:
ear
Set 15

Answer:
her
Set 15

Answer:
ear
Set 15

Answer:
her
Set 15

Answer:
ear
Set 15

GA1143

GA1143

Answer:

Set:

Answer:

Set:

Answer:

Set:

Answer:

Set:

Answer:

Set:

Answer:

Set:

Answer:

Set:

Answer:

Set:

Answer:

Set:

Answer:

Set:

Answer:

Set:

Answer:

Set:

Answer:

Set:

Answer:

Set:

Answer:

Set:

Answer:

Set:

Answer:

Set:

Answer:

Set:

Answer:

Set:

Answer:

Set:

GA1143

a	**b**	**c**
d	**e**	**f**
g	**h**	**i**
j	**k**	**l**
m	**n**	**o**
p	**q**	**r**
s	**t**	**u**

GA1143

V	**W**	**X**
Y	**Z**	**A**
B	**C**	**D**
E	**F**	**G**
H	**I**	**J**
K	**L**	**M**
N	**O**	**P**

GA1143

Shortcuts for
Teaching Phonics
Good Apple, Inc.
by Flora Joy
© 1990

Shortcuts for
Teaching Phonics
Good Apple, Inc.
by Flora Joy
© 1990

Shortcuts for
Teaching Phonics
Good Apple, Inc.
by Flora Joy
© 1990

Shortcuts for
Teaching Phonics
Good Apple, Inc.
by Flora Joy
© 1990

Shortcuts for
Teaching Phonics
Good Apple, Inc.
by Flora Joy
© 1990

Shortcuts for
Teaching Phonics
Good Apple, Inc.
by Flora Joy
© 1990

Shortcuts for
Teaching Phonics
Good Apple, Inc.
by Flora Joy
© 1990

Shortcuts for
Teaching Phonics
Good Apple, Inc.
by Flora Joy
© 1990

Shortcuts for
Teaching Phonics
Good Apple, Inc.
by Flora Joy
© 1990

Shortcuts for
Teaching Phonics
Good Apple, Inc.
by Flora Joy
© 1990

Shortcuts for
Teaching Phonics
Good Apple, Inc.
by Flora Joy
© 1990

Shortcuts for
Teaching Phonics
Good Apple, Inc.
by Flora Joy
© 1990

Shortcuts for
Teaching Phonics
Good Apple, Inc.
by Flora Joy
© 1990

Shortcuts for
Teaching Phonics
Good Apple, Inc.
by Flora Joy
© 1990

Shortcuts for
Teaching Phonics
Good Apple, Inc.
by Flora Joy
© 1990

Shortcuts for
Teaching Phonics
Good Apple, Inc.
by Flora Joy
© 1990

Shortcuts for
Teaching Phonics
Good Apple, Inc.
by Flora Joy
© 1990

Shortcuts for
Teaching Phonics
Good Apple, Inc.
by Flora Joy
© 1990

GA1143

Q	R	S
T	U	V
W	X	Y
Z	-ai-	-au-
-aw-	-ay-	-ea-
-ee-	-ei-	-ey-
-oa-	-oi-	-oo-

GA1143

Shortcuts for
Teaching Phonics
Good Apple, Inc.
by Flora Joy
© 1990

Shortcuts for
Teaching Phonics
Good Apple, Inc.
by Flora Joy
© 1990

Shortcuts for
Teaching Phonics
Good Apple, Inc.
by Flora Joy
© 1990

Shortcuts for
Teaching Phonics
Good Apple, Inc.
by Flora Joy
© 1990

Shortcuts for
Teaching Phonics
Good Apple, Inc.
by Flora Joy
© 1990

Shortcuts for
Teaching Phonics
Good Apple, Inc.
by Flora Joy
© 1990

Shortcuts for
Teaching Phonics
Good Apple, Inc.
by Flora Joy
© 1990

Shortcuts for
Teaching Phonics
Good Apple, Inc.
by Flora Joy
© 1990

Shortcuts for
Teaching Phonics
Good Apple, Inc.
by Flora Joy
© 1990

Shortcuts for
Teaching Phonics
Good Apple, Inc.
by Flora Joy
© 1990

Shortcuts for
Teaching Phonics
Good Apple, Inc.
by Flora Joy
© 1990

Shortcuts for
Teaching Phonics
Good Apple, Inc.
by Flora Joy
© 1990

Shortcuts for
Teaching Phonics
Good Apple, Inc.
by Flora Joy
© 1990

Shortcuts for
Teaching Phonics
Good Apple, Inc.
by Flora Joy
© 1990

Shortcuts for
Teaching Phonics
Good Apple, Inc.
by Flora Joy
© 1990

Shortcuts for
Teaching Phonics
Good Apple, Inc.
by Flora Joy
© 1990

Shortcuts for
Teaching Phonics
Good Apple, Inc.
by Flora Joy
© 1990

Shortcuts for
Teaching Phonics
Good Apple, Inc.
by Flora Joy
© 1990

GA1143

-ou-	-ow-	-oy-
-ar-	-er-	-ir-
-or-	-ur-	bl-
br-	ch-	cl-
cr-	dr-	fl-
fr-	gh-	gl-
gr-	kn-	ph-

GA1143

Shortcuts for
Teaching Phonics
Good Apple, Inc.
by Flora Joy
© 1990

Shortcuts for
Teaching Phonics
Good Apple, Inc.
by Flora Joy
© 1990

Shortcuts for
Teaching Phonics
Good Apple, Inc.
by Flora Joy
© 1990

Shortcuts for
Teaching Phonics
Good Apple, Inc.
by Flora Joy
© 1990

Shortcuts for
Teaching Phonics
Good Apple, Inc.
by Flora Joy
© 1990

Shortcuts for
Teaching Phonics
Good Apple, Inc.
by Flora Joy
© 1990

Shortcuts for
Teaching Phonics
Good Apple, Inc.
by Flora Joy
© 1990

Shortcuts for
Teaching Phonics
Good Apple, Inc.
by Flora Joy
© 1990

Shortcuts for
Teaching Phonics
Good Apple, Inc.
by Flora Joy
© 1990

Shortcuts for
Teaching Phonics
Good Apple, Inc.
by Flora Joy
© 1990

Shortcuts for
Teaching Phonics
Good Apple, Inc.
by Flora Joy
© 1990

Shortcuts for
Teaching Phonics
Good Apple, Inc.
by Flora Joy
© 1990

Shortcuts for
Teaching Phonics
Good Apple, Inc.
by Flora Joy
© 1990

Shortcuts for
Teaching Phonics
Good Apple, Inc.
by Flora Joy
© 1990

Shortcuts for
Teaching Phonics
Good Apple, Inc.
by Flora Joy
© 1990

Shortcuts for
Teaching Phonics
Good Apple, Inc.
by Flora Joy
© 1990

Shortcuts for
Teaching Phonics
Good Apple, Inc.
by Flora Joy
© 1990

Shortcuts for
Teaching Phonics
Good Apple, Inc.
by Flora Joy
© 1990

GA1143

pl-	**pr-**	**sc-**
scr-	**sh-**	**sl-**
sm-	**sn-**	**sp-**
spl-	**spr-**	**st-**
str-	**sw-**	**th-**
thr-	**tr-**	**tw-**
wh-	**wr-**	**-ab**

GA1143

Shortcuts for
Teaching Phonics
Good Apple, Inc.
by Flora Joy
© 1990

Shortcuts for
Teaching Phonics
Good Apple, Inc.
by Flora Joy
© 1990

Shortcuts for
Teaching Phonics
Good Apple, Inc.
by Flora Joy
© 1990

Shortcuts for
Teaching Phonics
Good Apple, Inc.
by Flora Joy
© 1990

Shortcuts for
Teaching Phonics
Good Apple, Inc.
by Flora Joy
© 1990

Shortcuts for
Teaching Phonics
Good Apple, Inc.
by Flora Joy
© 1990

Shortcuts for
Teaching Phonics
Good Apple, Inc.
by Flora Joy
© 1990

Shortcuts for
Teaching Phonics
Good Apple, Inc.
by Flora Joy
© 1990

Shortcuts for
Teaching Phonics
Good Apple, Inc.
by Flora Joy
© 1990

Shortcuts for
Teaching Phonics
Good Apple, Inc.
by Flora Joy
© 1990

Shortcuts for
Teaching Phonics
Good Apple, Inc.
by Flora Joy
© 1990

Shortcuts for
Teaching Phonics
Good Apple, Inc.
by Flora Joy
© 1990

Shortcuts for
Teaching Phonics
Good Apple, Inc.
by Flora Joy
© 1990

Shortcuts for
Teaching Phonics
Good Apple, Inc.
by Flora Joy
© 1990

Shortcuts for
Teaching Phonics
Good Apple, Inc.
by Flora Joy
© 1990

Shortcuts for
Teaching Phonics
Good Apple, Inc.
by Flora Joy
© 1990

Shortcuts for
Teaching Phonics
Good Apple, Inc.
by Flora Joy
© 1990

Shortcuts for
Teaching Phonics
Good Apple, Inc.
by Flora Joy
© 1990

GA1143

-ace	-ack	-ad
-ade	-ag	-ail
-ain	-ake	-all
-am	-ame	-amp
-an	-and	-ane
-ang	-ank	-ap
-are	-ark	-ash

GA1143

Shortcuts for Teaching Phonics
Good Apple, Inc.
by Flora Joy
© 1990

GA1143

-at	-ate	-ave
-ead	-eak	-eal
-eam	-ear	-eat
-ed	-eed	-eep
-eet	-ell	-en
-end	-ent	-est
-et	-ew	-ice

Shortcuts for
Teaching Phonics
Good Apple, Inc.
by Flora Joy
© 1990

Shortcuts for
Teaching Phonics
Good Apple, Inc.
by Flora Joy
© 1990

Shortcuts for
Teaching Phonics
Good Apple, Inc.
by Flora Joy
© 1990

Shortcuts for
Teaching Phonics
Good Apple, Inc.
by Flora Joy
© 1990

Shortcuts for
Teaching Phonics
Good Apple, Inc.
by Flora Joy
© 1990

Shortcuts for
Teaching Phonics
Good Apple, Inc.
by Flora Joy
© 1990

Shortcuts for
Teaching Phonics
Good Apple, Inc.
by Flora Joy
© 1990

Shortcuts for
Teaching Phonics
Good Apple, Inc.
by Flora Joy
© 1990

Shortcuts for
Teaching Phonics
Good Apple, Inc.
by Flora Joy
© 1990

Shortcuts for
Teaching Phonics
Good Apple, Inc.
by Flora Joy
© 1990

Shortcuts for
Teaching Phonics
Good Apple, Inc.
by Flora Joy
© 1990

Shortcuts for
Teaching Phonics
Good Apple, Inc.
by Flora Joy
© 1990

Shortcuts for
Teaching Phonics
Good Apple, Inc.
by Flora Joy
© 1990

Shortcuts for
Teaching Phonics
Good Apple, Inc.
by Flora Joy
© 1990

Shortcuts for
Teaching Phonics
Good Apple, Inc.
by Flora Joy
© 1990

Shortcuts for
Teaching Phonics
Good Apple, Inc.
by Flora Joy
© 1990

Shortcuts for
Teaching Phonics
Good Apple, Inc.
by Flora Joy
© 1990

Shortcuts for
Teaching Phonics
Good Apple, Inc.
by Flora Joy
© 1990

GA1143

-ick	-id	-ide
-ig	-ight	-ill
-im	-ime	-in
-ind	-ine	-ing
-ink	-int	-ip
-it	-ive	-ob
-ock	-od	-og

GA1143

GA1143

-oke	-old	-one
-ong	-oom	-oon
-op	-ope	-ore
-orn	-ot	-ub
-uff	-ug	-um
-ump	-un	-ung
-unk	-ush	-ut

Shortcuts for
Teaching Phonics
Good Apple, Inc.
by Flora Joy
© *1990*

Shortcuts for
Teaching Phonics
Good Apple, Inc.
by Flora Joy
© *1990*

Shortcuts for
Teaching Phonics
Good Apple, Inc.
by Flora Joy
© *1990*

Shortcuts for
Teaching Phonics
Good Apple, Inc.
by Flora Joy
© *1990*

Shortcuts for
Teaching Phonics
Good Apple, Inc.
by Flora Joy
© *1990*

Shortcuts for
Teaching Phonics
Good Apple, Inc.
by Flora Joy
© *1990*

Shortcuts for
Teaching Phonics
Good Apple, Inc.
by Flora Joy
© *1990*

Shortcuts for
Teaching Phonics
Good Apple, Inc.
by Flora Joy
© *1990*

Shortcuts for
Teaching Phonics
Good Apple, Inc.
by Flora Joy
© *1990*

Shortcuts for
Teaching Phonics
Good Apple, Inc.
by Flora Joy
© *1990*

Shortcuts for
Teaching Phonics
Good Apple, Inc.
by Flora Joy
© *1990*

Shortcuts for
Teaching Phonics
Good Apple, Inc.
by Flora Joy
© *1990*

Shortcuts for
Teaching Phonics
Good Apple, Inc.
by Flora Joy
© *1990*

Shortcuts for
Teaching Phonics
Good Apple, Inc.
by Flora Joy
© *1990*

Shortcuts for
Teaching Phonics
Good Apple, Inc.
by Flora Joy
© *1990*

Shortcuts for
Teaching Phonics
Good Apple, Inc.
by Flora Joy
© *1990*

Shortcuts for
Teaching Phonics
Good Apple, Inc.
by Flora Joy
© *1990*

Shortcuts for
Teaching Phonics
Good Apple, Inc.
by Flora Joy
© *1990*

GA1143

GA1143

Tab Items for Mini-Card Activities

Items for Phonics Question Mini-Cards

b- d- t- g-

Long i Short i

br- cr- -ck -st

ee ea ou ow 1 2 1 2

Long Short Hard c Soft c

Hard g Soft g good food

wed weed ear her

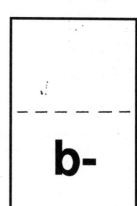

Paste items onto small cards and fold:

b-

Items for File Dividers

Set 1   Set 2
Set 3   Set 4
Set 5   Set 6
Set 7   Set 8
Set 9   Set 10

Single Letters
Vowel Teams
Consonant Teams
Phonograms

Examples:

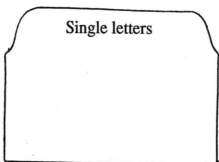

Single letters

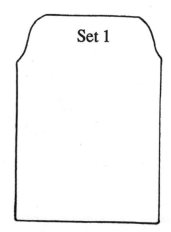

Set 1

GA1143